Yours truly

G. W. Arrington

GEORGE

WASHINGTON

ARRINGTON

Civil War Spy, Texas Ranger,
Sheriff and Rancher

A Biography

By Jerry Sinise

Copyright 1979
By Jerry Sinise

Published in the United States of America
By Eakin Press, P.O. Box 178, Burnet, Texas 78611

ALL RIGHTS RESERVED

ISBN 0-89015-216-0

ii

DEDICATION

To my wife Dorothy
This is the second one.

By the same author:

Pink Higgins, The Reluctant Gunfighter
Nortex Press, 1973

PREFACE

It is unfortunate that recent generations have no heroes. When I was a youngster, I had dozens to choose from—Daniel Boone, Davy Crockett, Kit Carson, Jack Armstrong, the Lone Ranger and Tonto, the Shadow, Doc Savage, Superman and G-8. While my childish imagination made these American folk heroes larger than life, they also gave me a feeling that all was right in this country as long as these defenders of justice were combating the evils of the world.

And even in a day when "reality" tends to cut this nation's giants down to more human proportions, they still are the heroes I want·them to be.

George Washington (Cap) Arrington has to be numbered among the giants who won the West. He is, to me anyway, a hero's hero. I became interested in him when I read on his granite headstone in the Mobeetie, Tex. cemetery:

Captain G.W. Arrington
Dec. 23, 1844—March 31, 1923
A Daring Scout in Colonel Mosby's Command
During the Civil War
Captain of Company C of the Texas Rangers
Sheriff of Wheeler and Attached Counties
for Eight Years
A Fearless Officer to Whom the Frontier of
Texas Owes a Debt of Gratitude

He sounded unbelievable! And now that I have finished writing what I was able to find about him, he still is.

To avoid some first chapter confusion, Arrington's real name was John Cromwell Orrick Jr. He changed his name to Arrington during the Civil War, interchanging it with Orrick. He changed it finally to Arrington following his shooting of a Negro in his hometown of Greensboro, Ala.

His exploits were awesome. He was a man among men. Soldier, spy, Texas Ranger, sheriff, rancher, from the start of the Civil War to the opening of the Texas frontier to the settling of the Texas Panhandle, a period of time when survival was a man's first consideration. His years as a Ranger were dangerous ones in the Frontier Battalion. His days as sheriff rival any of those of the Earps and the Mastersons. What else can be said about a man who was a part of many of the West's maturing years?

Many people helped (and some hindered) in gathering material for this brief biography of the man who brought law and order to the Texas Panhandle. There is always the danger of leaving someone out in naming names, and this certainly is not intentional. Most helpful were the late French Arrington and his charming wife, Ollie, Canadian, Tex.; William L. Arrington, Pampa, Tex.; Ben Stone Jr., Amarillo, Tex. attorney; Tom Hill, Hemphill County and District Clerk, Canadian, Tex.; Lawrence Yeager, Greensboro, Ala.; Woods Coffey Jr., Dumas, Tex.; Dr. George Beto and Henry Small, Bureau of Records and Identification, Texas Department of Corrections, Huntsville, Tex.

Also Mrs. Irene Simpson Neasham, director, Wells Fargo Bank History Room, San Francisco, Calif.; Milo B. Howard Jr., director, State of Alabama Department of Archives and History, Birmingham, Ala.; Robert D. Dortch, director of admissions and records, Birmingham-Southern College, Birmingham.

And the Southwest Collection, Texas Tech University, Lubbock; The Texas State Library, Austin, Tex.; National Archives and Records Service, Washington, D.C.; San Antonio Express, San Antonio, Tex.; The Adjutant General's Office, Austin, Tex.; The University of Texas Archives, Austin, Tex.; Fort Worth Library; Mary E. Bivins Memorial Library, Amarillo, Tex.; and the Panhandle-Plains Museum, Canyon, Tex.

G. W. (CAP) ARRINGTON (whose real name was John C. Orrick, Jr.) at age 16½ in his Confederate Army uniform. A rare photo owned by his grandson, William Arrington, Pampa, Texas.

COMMANDS ARRINGTON
SERVED WITH
1861 TO 1865

Enlisted Confederate Army, April 13, 1861
Left home May 5, 1861, for Virginia.
Company I, Fifth Alabama Infantry.

Company D, Fifth Alabama Infantry.
Company E, Jeff Davis Legion, Hampton's Brigade, Stuart's Cavalry.

Company C, Mosby's Partisan Rangers, 43rd Virginia Battalion, Army Northern Virginia, Robert E. Lee, Commanding General.

Paroled April 29, 1865, by General Chapman, USA, near Berryville, Va.

TABLE OF CONTENTS

ILLUSTRATIONS

Frontispiece: G. W. (Capt) Arrington

George

Washington

Arrington

CERTIFY, That the within named _Jno C. Orrick_ a _Private_ of Captain _J W Williams_ Company, _"D"_ of the _Fifth_ Regiment of _Alabama_, born in _Greene Co._ in the State of _Alabama_, aged _17_ years, _5_ feet, _5_ inches high, _light_ complexion, _black_ eyes, _light_ hair, and by occupation _Student_ was enlisted by _Capt J A Jones_ at _Greensboro Ala_ on the _13th_ day of _April_ 186_1_, to serve _One_ year, and is now entitled to discharge by reason of _Being under 18 Years of age and not liable to Military Service_

The said _J. C. Orrick_ was last paid by _Maj Jno Ambler_ to include the _31st_ day of _May_ 1862, and has pay due from that date to the present date.

There is due to him _____ ₁₀₀ Dollars traveling allowance from _____, the place of discharge, to _____, the place of enrolment, transportation not being furnished in kind.

There is due him _Twenty five $ for Commutation Clothing 1st & mos 2nd Year_

He is indebted to the Confederate States _nothing_ ₁₀₀ Dollars on account of _____

Given in duplicate at _Richmond Va_, this _18th_ day of _August_ 186_2_.

J. W. Williams
Capt Commanding Company. _"D"_
5th Regt Ala

ACCOUNT TO BE MADE BY QUARTERMASTER.

NOTE.—When this certificate is transferred, it must be on the back, witnessed by a Commissioned Officer, if practicable, or by some other reputable person well known to the Quartermaster.

For pay from _1st_ of _Jany_ 186_2_, to _1st_ of _August_ 186_2_, being _2_ months and _18_ days, at _Eleven_ Dollars per month, - - - | 2 5 | 6 0 |

For pay for traveling from _____ to _____, being _____ miles, at ten cents per mile, - - - | 1 2 | 5 0 |

Clothing Amount, - - | 4 1 | 1 0 |

Deduct for clothing overdrawn, _Clothing_ _____

Balance paid, - - - | | |

RECEIVED of _Capt John Mason_ C.S. Army, this _8_ day of _Aug_ 186_2_, _fifty one_ Dollars and _10_ Cents, in full of the above account.

(Signed duplicates.) _J. C. Orrick_

WITNESS:

THE ENLISTMENT RECORD showing the date John C. Orrick (G.W. (Cap) Arrington) first enlisted in the Confederate Army. The date was April 13, 1861, and he was to serve one year. He was under 18 years of age and not liable to military service. However, he remained in the army until the War was over.

1

CHAPTER ONE

A Spy With The Gray Ghost

The two men, wearing dusty jackets of Union blue, rode slowly out of the thick Maryland woods toward a nearby house. The only sounds above the twittering birds were the clopping hoofs of their horses on the powder-dry road and the creak of leather as the two shifted to fit themselves comfortably in their worn saddles. Three gentlemen, one a minister, watched their approach from the broad board porch.

"Mornin'," one of the soldiers said.

"Morning," returned the three, cautious but friendly. "Set awhile."

The two climbed down off their somewhat jaded mounts and walked stiff-legged to seats on the porch. The men offered the travel-stained soldiers a gladly-accepted snack.

During the unhurried conversation about the war, one of their hosts, warning the two to be on the lookout, observed that the spy "Orrick is scouting in the neighborhood."

"Can you describe him?" one of the soldiers asked, interested.

Small, slight build, five feet five or six. Maybe 120 or 130 pounds. No more than a boy.

Having finished their meal, the two strangers, who had told their hosts they were from Chicago, arose, and Orrick, permitting himself a slight smile, introduced himself to his dumbfounded hosts.

"Thank you," he said. "We found out one thing we wanted to know. Our presence in Maryland is known. Now if you'd be so kind as to provide us with provisions for our companions in those woods over there." Their shaken hosts sacked up what food was available and handed it to the smiling spies.

As the two walked out on the porch, they looked down the road away from the house and woods and spotted a cloud of dust a half mile distant. Bidding their hosts goodby, they put spurs to their horses and headed back toward the woods. Their hosts, standing on the porch, heard their laughter just before they disappeared into the thick brush and trees.

Union cavalry, making enough noise to be heard minutes away, charged up to the house and the three men.

"That way!" the three pointed, and the cavalry rode off on a fruitless search for the Confederate spies on Union soil.

For nearly two years, July 1863 to April 1865, John Cromwell Orrick Jr. was with John S. Mosby, the Gray Ghost of the Confederacy, dubbed by the North as the "blackest of redoubtable scoun-

2

drels," "land pirate," "horse thief," "murderer," and the one
Mosby liked most of all, "guerilla."

Orrick, four months past his eighteenth birthday when he joined
Mosby following a remarkable escape from a Federal prison train,
was already a seasoned soldier of two years. He had enlisted as a
private in Company I, 5th Alabama Infantry, on April 13, 1861,
the day following the opening gun of the Civil War. Orrick was
16½ years old, and was among the 209 men of Company I, led by
Captain Allen C. Jones.

The company left Greensboro, Alabama on May 1, 1861, for
Manassas, a small railroad settlement a few miles east of the Bull
Run Mountains in Virginia, 25 miles southwest of Washington,
D.C. The Alabamians became a part of The Army of the Shenan-
doah under General Joseph E. Johnston.

The first battle at Manassas began at 5:15 a.m., July 21, 1861,
with the firing of a 30-pounder Parrot rifle by artillerymen of Brigadier General Daniel Tyler's command, the Union Army's First
Division. There were large quantities of provisions and munitions
stored at the rail junction, feebly guarded, and a small number,
less than five hundred, Alabamians, Georgians and North Carol-
inians, volunteered to march to the rail station. Among the volunteers was young Orrick.

Orrick in later life never talked much about his baptism of fire.
He would remind his listeners only that "the South won the
battle."

Before the seesaw battle was finished on the afternoon of July
22, the Union, which committed its First, Second, Third, Fourth
and Fifth Divisions, approximately 35,000 men, to the fight, lost
460 killed, 1,124 wounded and 1,312 captured or missing. The
South, winner of the first round, committed its Army of the Potomac (9,713 men of 21,900 available) and Army of the Shenan-
doah, 8,340 men. The Confederacy lost 387, had 1,582 wounded
and 13 captured or missing.

News of the victory flashed through the Confederacy. Thanks-
giving sermons were preached, public officials issued congratula-
tory proclamations and many Southerners were of the opinion the
war was over. A false sense of security developed in the South,
and this in itself was more damaging than was the disaster of defeat for the North.

Preliminary skirmishes heralding the start of the second battle
at Manassas began August 27, 1861, and the main battle was
joined August 29, with the decisive battle being fought on August
30. The Union lost this one, too. Confederate forces numering
55,000 soundly trounced a Union army of 73,000. The North lost
1,747 men; the South, 1,553.

3

Company I became Company D, 5th Regiment, Alabama Infantry, and Orrick, now a few months older than 17, fought with this company at least through the Battle of Seven Pines, May 31 and June 1, 1862, where 27 men died and 128 were wounded; the Seven Days battles before Richmond during the latter part of June, and at Sharpsburg, September 17, where he was wounded for the first time.

The 5th Alabama, part of Archer's Brigade, commanded by Brigadier General James J. Archer, was active in the Maryland Campaign, which included Harper's Ferry, Antietam and Shepherdstown. Captain Charles M. Hooper was in command of the 5th Alabama.

Exactly what happened to the 5th Alabama during the indecisive battle at Sharpsburg was not determined. More than 100,000 men, both Union and Confederate, fought in, around and about the small community. It could have been that the 5th Alabama was absorbed by other units when the battle finally ended. A few months following this major battle, Orrick was listed as a private in Company E, Jeff Davis Legion of Cavalry. He was with this company during the fighting at Gettysburg.

The main battle at Gettysburg, said to have been the "greatest battle fought in the Western Hemisphere," began July 1, 1863. For three days, more than 163,000 men waged a vicious, unyielding fight. The battle ended in disaster for the South on July 3, and the decimated Southern army retreated in confusion, fighting small skirmishes along the way.

Official Confederate reports listed Orrick as "missing in action since 10 July 1863 at Funkstown, Md," and "killed 11 July at Funkstown, Md." Funkstown, located near Hagerstown, Md., and a short distance from Gettysburg, was a small community on the retreat route.

Orrick, however, had been captured, not killed, and was put on a Federal prison train for confinement at Fort McHenry near Baltimore.

Orrick was tired, dirty. His gunshot wound from the Sharpsburg battle was bothering him. He tried to find a place to sit among the weary, shell-shocked prisoners, jammed tightly into wooden cattle cars. The retreat was demoralizing, and other than the groans of the wounded, no one said much of anything.

The long train wound its way slowly southeast from Funkstown, where he had been captured, toward Baltimore. Orrick's body may have been tired, but his mind was not. He had relatives on a farm near Baltimore, and the first chance he got, he was going to get off this slow-moving train and head for his grandparents' place.

4

Just before the train rolled into Baltimore; Orrick, and a few others with similar ideas, made a break for freedom. He caught his captors napping and jumped off the train into thick brush and headed away from the train. A few shots cut the limbs above his head. The train rolled to a stop, and several of the blue-coated soldiers took out after him.

"This way!" one yelled. "Through those trees," another called out. "There he goes!" They punctuated their shouts with rifle shots.

Orrick ran this way and that, always watching behind to see how close his followers were. His wound opened. Blood flowed freely, and he jammed part of his shirt into the hole. He ran for his life.

"There's one!" someone called in the distance. A shot rang out. A scream. One of his fellow escapees would never see the dawn. Orrick ran harder, faster. Up a hill. Down a hill. Through thick brush. Out in the open. His grandfather's farm was not far away. Sanctuary! The sounds of his pursuers faded. He hoped they had lost his trail, but knew that they would soon pick up the chase again. He did not have time to do too many fancy things in trying to throw them off.

Not much farther now. Exhausted, he leaned against a tree, breathing deeply. Off to his right, he heard something or someone moving heavily through the brush. He tensed. No one was going to take him back to that prison train. The sound was louder. Orrick looked around for a weapon, a stick, a rock, anything. Then, he visibly relaxed, relieved, and a nervous chuckle escaped from his dry lips. A cow. Just a cow! He looked around then, spotting a familiar clump of trees, a path he had walked down. He was on his grandfather's land.

"Go 'way! We don't want you here!"

Orrick could hardly believe what he was hearing.

"We're not going to hide you! If you're around here when the soldiers come, we'll turn you in!"

His grandparents turned him away. So much for family being more important than ideals. Orrick, hardened by more than a year of death, trials beyond all understanding, stared at his grandfather, trying to grasp what was beyond all reason. Then, without a word, he headed back toward the woods. The memory of that moment was never forgotten.

His blue-jacketed pursuers never caught him. He eluded them at every turn and finally reached the Virginia shore in Loudoun County. Speaking of the escape years following the event, some of Orrick's companions said it was "one of the most daring of the war."

On the April 30 to August 31, 1864 muster roll of Company E, Jeff Davis Legion of Cavalry, Orrick was listed as "absent without leave, known to be with Mosby's command." He was in Company C, Mosby's Rangers, 43rd Virginia Battalion.

While Col. John Singleton Mosby contributed little to influence the main war, his rangers confused the enemy in a campaign of underground activity that brought stature and romance to this particular mode of warfare. Mosby was a nagging thorn in the side of the Federals, and they did all they could to exorcise this "gray ghost" of Loudoun Valley, his main area of operation.

Mosby, born December 6, 1833, in Powhatan County, Va., was an attorney by profession, and when the war began enlisted as a private in the Confederate cavalry. By the time the Battle of Gettysburg was fought, he was a colonel and a plague to General Sheridan.

His guerillas destroyed supply trains, isolated troops from their bases, captured dispatches, cut communications and neutralized as many as 50,000 Union troops by forcing them to guard their rear and their capital.

Orrick's adventures with Mosby were legendary, and in Mosby's later years in Washington, the cavalry leader was to remember Orrick with fondness as a man after his own heart.

Major John Scott, Mosby's adjutant, wrote of Orrick in 1867: "He is a good soldier, is cool and brave, and, being well acquainted in Maryland, is often employed by his commander to obtain information from that side of the Potomac."

Orrick and four others crossed the Potomac below Leesburg, Va., and spent the night in the woods near Middlebrook, stationing themselves along a road leading into that small community.

Shortly following sunrise, the five spotted a traveler in civilian dress horseback. Orrick took note of the rider's army saddle and large brass spurs. The men, rifles pointed, stepped out of the brush and ordered the man to surrender. Their sudden appearance caused the man to rein sharply, pulling the horse sideways in the road.

"Don't shoot!" he shouted.

Orrick motioned him down off his horse, and the man, spurs jangling, hastily climbed down. He hung onto the reins with shaking hands.

"I'm nobody," he cried. "Nobody. Let me go, please. I'm a Democrat, and that should mean something."

Orrick snorted. "I don't see much difference between a War Democrat and a Republican." Turning to one of his companions, he told him to take his horse and the pistols the man was wearing.

"Who are you and where you going?" Orrick wanted to know.

"A clerk. Just a sutler's clerk. I'm headed for Frederick City."

Orrick questioned him further, but decided the man was as harmless as he appeared.

"Let him go. I doubt that the Federal army will gain much strength from War Democrats of that pattern."

The man boarded his horse and rode quickly off, looking over his shoulder a time or two to make sure the guerillas had not changed their minds. The five chuckled as they watched his frightened departure.

Leaving his companions, Orrick, dressed in civilian clothes, rode into Baltimore, picking up vital information during his brief stay. On the way out, he stopped and entered a sparsely stocked mercantile store and purchased gray cloth for a uniform and other articles useful to the Ranger service he was in.

Federal soldiers stopped him on the way out of town, but he answered their questions satisfactorily, and was allowed to ride on. Once out of sight, he kicked his horse into a mile-eating gallop and headed back to his Ranger camp in a heavily wooded area away from the Maryland city.

That same night the Rangers started for Montgomery County. Orrick had the point.

They passed a frame house filled with hay. Around it a number of horses were eating. Orrick, in front, rode up to them under the impression they were colts. Then he spotted about twenty blue coats asleep on the ground. He wheeled his horse, but in doing so, he rode over a plank, and the sharp sound awakened the Union soldiers. They grabbed their rifles and began to pursue the hard riding Rangers.

The fugitives urged their horses on, crashing through the woods this way and that. An occasional rifle shot was heard, but none of the balls came close. Sounds of pursuit died out, and the Rangers, after a run of some five miles, pulled up, allowing their horses a breather.

"Pull off the side of the road," Orrick ordered.

The Confederates, hearing the sound of hoofs pounding down the road, turned into the wood until the Yankees charged by.

"Since we're traveling in the same direction, let's act as rear guard," someone suggested. The Rangers laughed at that, and kicked their tired mounts into slow pursuit of their pursuers.

Orrick and his companions rode into Darnestown, and the Alabamian went to the house of a citizen in search of information. He was asked inside, and while he was talking with the young ladies of the family, a knock was heard at the door.

CAP ARRINGTON probably in his 20s. This rare photo, owned by William Arrington, Pampa, Tex., shows Cap smoking one of his occasional cigars. It is not known when or where the photo was taken.

Orrick and the girls stood perfectly still, shocked by the knock. One of the girls pointed frantically toward some stairs, and Orrick ran into an adjoining room, up the staircase. One of the girls followed him.

Silently, in near panic, she motioned toward an old-fashioned chest in one of the upstairs rooms. Orrick, with little ceremony, concealed himself in the chest. The girl put a large box on the lid, and, composing herself, walked out of the room, down the stairs to where the Federal soldiers were questioning her sisters.

"No. We've not seen any Confederates," one sister was saying.

"Well, ma'am," the Union officer said, "we know Rangers are in the area. Do you mind if we look around?" And without waiting for her answer, he gestured to the soldiers behind him. They started a room by room search.

Orrick, in the cramped closeness of the chest, heard the soldiers walk by.

"Nothing here," one said. "Try that closet." Their voices faded in and out as they went from room to room. Then there was silence.

Orrick could not stand it any longer. His circulation was slowing, and his legs were going to sleep. He put both hands on the chest lid and shoved. The big box crashed noisily to the floor. Drawing his pistol, he crept quickly to the head of the stairs, fully assured that in that position he would be a match for his assailants.

He saw the girls looking out of the windows. One turned. "They're riding away." They all breathed somewhat easier.

Orrick thanked the ladies, joined his friends and recrossed the Potomac with the information the young women had provided.

There were other adventures and narrow escapes, fire fights with Union soldiers, but the War was grinding to a stop with defeat following defeat on all fronts of the South and West.

On April 9, 1865, Lee met Grant in the front parlor of Wilmer McLean's Appomattox farmhouse, and Lee accepted the generous terms offered by the North. The actual surrender ceremony took place April 12 "when 28,231 exhausted Confederates representing the Army of Northern Virginia relinquished their arms and battle flags." A Federal general, deeply moved by the scene, described it as "an awed stillness, and breath-holding, as if it were the passing of the dead."

Mosby disbanded his guerillas on April 21, 1865, and through the influence of General Grant, was pardoned. He returned to his law practice, joined the Republican Party and canvassed Virginia when Grant ran for president in 1872. Mosby's parole caused quite a stir in the North, but Grant stood behind it. Horace Greeley, an outspoken newspaper editor, called Mosby "a guerilla and a murderer," and published story after story asking the president to hang him. Mosby, harrassed beyond all reason, fled and said he would fight to the very end. Mrs. Mosby went to Grant and asked his help, and Grant said that if Mosby would surrender, he would protect him. Mosby did and Grant was true to his word. Mosby never forgot it.

On April 29, 1865, Orrick was paroled by General Chapman, USA, near Berryville, Clark County, Virginia, and headed back to his home in Greensboro.

Three companies of the 11th Missouri Infantry, 300 men, were stationed in Greensboro to keep the peace when Orrick got there. But "peace" was a tenuous condition. The town felt it was at the mercy of the troops, carpetbaggers and scavengers. Tempers were short. Reconstruction, Orrick knew, was not going to be easy, and the policy pursued by the United States government during Reconstruction came very near completely wrecking all that was left in the South after the four years of war.

The shooting of a Union soldier nearly resulted in the burning and sacking of the town by the bluecoats.

On the morning of Aug. 31, 1865, three Federal soldiers entered the general store of Robert B. Waller Jr. and asked for some fruit. They stood around eating it, then, over the protests of Waller, walked out without paying for it. Waller, outraged, took the matter up with their company commander, and he in turn told the men to pay. They did, reluctantly.

But the three would not leave it alone. They returned to Waller's store and, without warning, one of the soldiers struck a young man who had seen considerable Confederate Army service across the face with a slung shot, mistaking him, it is supposed, for Waller.

The young man sprang to his feet, drew his pistol and fired. He missed. The Federals ran. The one who had hit the youth turned to see where he was, and the young soldier steadied his pistol, pulled the trigger, shooting the Union soldier in the head.

That did it! Soldiers from the nearby camp poured into town. The young Confederate, spotting a Thoroughbred racer tied to a nearby hitching rack, leaped into the saddle and headed out of town. The soldiers took off after him, but dropped far behind the fast-paced racer. They lost him a few miles out of Greensboro, and the next day, the Confederate crossed into Mississippi.

Then, the Union soldiers arrested the fugitive's brother.

"If we can't have the killer, we'll hang his brother," they shouted. "And we'll sack the town to boot!"

They set sundown as a deadline for delivering up the runaway killer. To bolster their courage, the soldiers confiscated all the whiskey they could find and drank themselves into a drunken rage.

"Where's the rope!?!" "Hang him here!"

They put the noose around the frightened boy's neck and dragged him to the front of the hotel his father operated. The rope was thrown over one end of a sign board. "Pull!" someone yelled.

Just then, a buggy behind two foam-flecked horses shoved its way through the shouting soldiers. Someone had ridden to Marion, Alabama, to get the regiment's colonel.

"Take that rope from around his neck," he ordered. "We still don't hang men without a trial."

The soldiers, in an ugly mood, murmured their disapproval. No one moved to remove the rope. There was indecision there, and it could go either way. The colonel drew his pistol and pointed it at the apparent ringleaders.

"I'm ordering you men to fall in, and I'll shoot the first man who refuses to obey." The snap of command and the discipline of years in the army worked. The rope was removed from the fugitive's brother's neck.

"We'll hold him prisoner until we can transfer him to Tuscaloosa, where he'll be tried for shooting a Federal soldier," the officer said. Apparently the young man had wounded a soldier during the shooting by his brother. The transfer was made. However, he escaped and was never recaptured.

Orrick was restless. The life of a merchant was too slow following his life as a spy and soldier. The war had been over nearly two years when Orrick and seven companions rode into Mexico to join the cause of Emperor Maximilian. The South supported the Austrian, seeing what he was doing as an extension of their own efforts in the States. The Archduke's power was waning, however, and Orrick and his friends arrived too late to join Maximilian's army as mercenaries.

Orrick returned home. On June 13, 1867, he killed Alex Webb, a Negro businessman. The *Alabama Beacon* dated June 15 had this story of the killing:

> **Homicide.**—Alex Webb, a colored man of this place was killed here last Thursday afternoon by Mr. John C. Orrick. The particulars of this tragic and deeply to be regretted affair, as we have heard them, are these: Orrick, who had been sitting for some time on a box in front of the store of Messrs. Jeffries, Johnston & Co., saw Alex Webb come down the flight of steps leading to Alex's shop, and advanced a few steps on a cross street and met Alex.— Then a few words passed between them,

11

which were not heard, so far as we have been able to learn, by any person,—Whereupon Orrick drew his pistol and fired three times, each shot taking effect, the last shot entering near the heart.—Alex fell dead and Orrick walked off up the street to his store, pistol in hand, remarking that "he would allow no damn negro to call him a damn liar."

We infer from the few facts we have been able to gather that something had previously passed between them through a third party, which was particularly offensive to Orrick.

Alex Webb, we take occasion to remark, was a man of good character, and had a large family dependent upon him for their support. The affair is most deeply regretted by the community. The Sheriff, who was in town at the time, promptly summoned a number of men and made search for Orrick, but did not find him. There was, we understand, a good deal of excitement among the colored people, some of them threatening to set fire to the town.

Webb, recently appointed one of the registers for the district of Hale and Greene Counties, was one of the leaders of his race during the Reconstruction period in Greensboro.

For three days, the Negroes in the small community paraded up and down the dusty, dirt main street. Some were armed with guns, knives, clubs. The whites prepared for the worst, but on Saturday afternoon, a company of U.S. troops (Company E, 33rd U.S. Infantry), commanded by Lt. F.P. Adams, rode into town, and things began to quiet down. The soldiers, with the help of the sheriff and sheriff's deputies, continued their search for Orrick.

Henry Peck, a Negro janitor at Southern University, helped him to escape. The story most often told is that Peck first hid Orrick in the university's basement, then moved him to the upper portion of the belfry, thinking it would be a safer place to hide. While he was in the belfry, the soldiers searched the building.

They came to the belfry, and while they searched below, Orrick slipped and fell. He grabbed frantically for anything to prevent him from falling on top of the soldiers below. His ring caught on a nail and held him. He did not dare move. The pressure on his ring finger was excrutiating. His finger began to bleed and the drops of blood fell onto the floor near the searching Federals. None noticed, and they finally moved on to search other rooms in the university.

AN EARLY PHOTO of G.W.
(Cap) Arrington.

MRS. G.W. ARRINGTON, age 22.
Her given name was Sarah.

Orrick, in pain, pulled himself up to safety. His ring finger, though badly cut, was in better condition than could be expected. He thought it was going to come off while he hung above the soldiers.

Peck, once the soldiers were gone, helped Orrick get to the Greensboro Cemetery, where one of the above-ground vaults provided an excellent hiding place. Orrick stayed there until he could locate a horse and escape from Greensboro. He left the States, stopping in Honduras, where apparently he remained more than a year.

Colonel John Harvey, editor of the *Alabama Beacon,* wrote in an editorial dated June 22, 1867:

> "Besides holding the absurd opinion that the citizens of Greensboro generally had some agency in the killing of Alex Webb, the colored people were greatly incensed against the whites because Orrick escaped. Now, during our residence in Greensboro, extending through a period of over 30 years, there have been quite a number of murders—probably a dozen or more—some of them of a most shocking character and if our memory serves us correctly, in but one instance was the murderer arrested soon after the occurrence. And in that case the murderer was so drunk when he perpetrated the crime that he scarcely knew what he was doing, and made no effort to escape. The arresting of a bold and determined man, fully armed, who had committed a murder, and who knows that his life would be endangered, if not certainly forfeited, by allowing himself to be taken, is an extremely hazardous business, which few men care to engage in. John C. Orrick was one of the boldest and most desperate men, when aroused, to be met with anywhere and we doubt if 50 men, summoned indiscriminately, could have taken him alive."

Orrick returned to the States during July, 1868, and traveled through Virginia, Maryland, Missouri and Arkansas, ending up in Galveston, Tex. in 1870. He had changed his name to George Washington Arrington, and was to be known by that name the remaining years of his life.

Arrington was his mother's maiden name. There are some indications he used the Arrington name during the Civil War in Confederate Service Records, also, possibly while spying in the North with Mosby.

His father, John C. Orrick Sr., married Miss Mariah (sometimes spelled Maria) Arrington on Feb. 11, 1841. The officiating minister was Rev. D.P. Bestor, pastor of the Salem Baptist Church. Orrick Sr., born Aug. 17, 1816, died Feb. 7, 1848, and his wife, following a proper period of mourning, married William Larkin Williams on Dec. 24, 1849. The Rev. E.V. LeVert, a Methodist minister, married them.

Williams, a dentist, was 48 years old, and his new wife, born in North Carolina, was 26. Her son, John C. Orrick Jr., was six. Williams is thought to have been killed during the War and buried in Virginia, his state of birth. Confederate records show that Williams enlisted as a private in Captain F.C. Barlow's Cavalry Company (Baldwin Rangers, 15th Confederate Cavalry) on May 12, 1862.

Orrick, four when his father died, was born Dec. 23, 1844, in Greensboro. He registered at Southern University in Greensboro on Oct. 8, 1860, with Williams as his guardian.

Southern University, chartered Jan. 26, 1856, opened its doors on Oct. 3, 1859, with five professors and Dr. William W. Wightman as president. Two students graduated with Bachelor of Arts degrees on July 4, 1860.

When war was declared, the faculty had considerable difficulty in preventing the boys from joining the army. The young men had been drilled for service, and they were ready. Orrick's name did not appear on the university's roll in 1861. He left school to join the army.

Following the murder of Webb, Orrick's escape to Central America and his return to the States as G.W. Arrington, the Alabamian, walked the 50 miles from Galveston to Houston and took a job in a sawmill. Then he went to work for the Houston and Texas Central Railroad, one of the state's most prosperous and heavily traveled lines. The H&TC's track extended from Houston to Navasota in Grimes County, a distance of 75 miles. Trains left Houston daily, except Sundays, at 10 a.m. and reached Hempstead, 50 miles away, at 2 p.m., connecting with the Washington County Railroad and tri-weekly stages from Brenham to Austin. The train arrived in Navasota about 4 p.m. and connected with tri-weekly coaches to Shreveport, then traveled on to Millican to connect with stages to Dallas and Waco.

Arrington then returned to Galveston, where he worked in a commission house until 1874. He then farmed in Collin County, and was hired to help trail a cattle herd to Brown County.

During April, 1875, he quit to join the Frontier Battalion.

BIBLIOGRAPHY

Chapter One

Birmingham-Southern College, Birmingham, Alabama, Registrar.

Civil War Times Illustrated, "The Guerilla War," Historical Times Inc., Gettysburg, Pa.

The Concise Illustrated History of the Civil War, American History Illustrated, a National Historical Society Publication.

Confederate Records, National Archives & Records Service, Washington, D.C.

Crucial Moments of the Civil War, Edited by Willard Webb, Bonanza Books, New York.

The Dark Corner of the Confederacy, Edited by B.P. Gallaway. Wm. C. Brown Book Co., Dubuque, Iowa, 1968.

The Greensboro Watchman, Greensboro, Alabama, August 29, 1963 issue.

The History of Greensboro, William Edward Wadsworth Yerby and Mabel Yerby Lawson, Colonial Press, Northport, Alabama, 1963.

Manassas (Bull Run), National Park Service Historical Handbook Series.

Marriage Book B, Greene County, Alabama, page 272.

Marriage Book C, Greene County, Alabama, Volume 154, page 35.

Partisan Life With Mosby, "John Orrick's Adventures," Harper & Brothers, New York, 1867.

State of Alabama Department of Archives & History.

AS FAR AS IS known this is the only photo of G.W. (Cap) Arrington and his company of Texas Rangers. Company C was organized in September, 1876. Arrington was a first lieutenant in Company C before becoming its captain. He led his men on many dangerous forays into Indian country. Cap Arrington is in the foreground in his shirt sleeves.

16

CHAPTER TWO

The Frontier Battalion

In 1874, the Texas Legislature passed a bill providing for the formation of six companies of 75 men each to be known as the Frontier Battalion, and on May 2, 1874, Gov. Richard Coke commissioned John B. Jones, a 39-year-old Corsicana rancher, to command the newly formed organization.

Jones, a man who never touched tobacco or liquor, but was addicted to coffee, had been in Terry's Rangers during the Civil War. He had joined this hard riding, hard fighting band of "Texicans" as a private, and within a few weeks was promoted to adjutant of the Fifteenth Texas Infantry.

Within 30 days of his commission, Major Jones had five companies of Texas Rangers in the field, and by July 10, all six companies were in service, protecting an area 400 miles long, 100 miles wide, from the Red River to the Nueces and southward to the Rio Grande. However, before Jones could station his Rangers strategically throughout the outlaw-plagued, Indian-terrorized area, he had to cut forces because of insufficient funds. He dropped six captains, six lieutenants and 270 men from the Battalion, leaving him with six companies of one lieutenant and 30 men each. Again the Legislature failed to come through with funds, and Jones disbanded one company on March 31, 1875, and another on April 30, 1875, leaving him with four companies totalling 124 men.

Texas' financial woes were evident in the near-bankrupt condition the State was in when Governor Coke and his Democrats ousted the State's carpetbagger governor, E.J. Davis, in 1874. The Panic of 1873 had resulted in financial chaos, and Coke found himself with the choice of allowing the State to sink ingloriously into a quagmire of unpaid bills or find new ways to generate operating funds. T.R. Fehrenbach in *Lone Star* wrote: "They chose to wield a radical knife. State expenditures were slashed without mercy. Salaries were cut, the school funds stopped, although both measures caused considerable anguish. . . . No way to reduce costs was ignored. A hundred other economies were introduced. These economies not only began to balance the budget, they dismantled government as a side-effect. The state treasury was able to go on a cash basis in 1879."

When June 1, 1875, rolled around, Major Jones was faced with a re-enlistment problem, and using all his persuasive powers, he managed to enlist four companies of one lieutenant and 40 men each to serve until September 1. In a letter to Colonel A.M. Hobby, adjutant general at Galveston, Jones wrote: "As there was no appropriation for frontier defense during these three months, I induced the men to serve without pay and take the chances of the next Legislature making an appropriation to pay them. By disbanding the two companies in March and April, we had saved enough of the last appropriation to pay for subsistence and forage."

Jones continued to build the Frontier Battalion, and by September 1, he had five companies. However, the Legislature's lack of response to the Battalion's need for funds forced him to reduce half of each company by December 1.

While cutting costs, the Legislature still looked toward the settling of the State. The Texans had claimed all lands north and east of the Rio Grande, as harsh and deadly an area as the Sahara Desert and as unknown. It was a land familiar to the Comanches, Kiowas and Mescalero Apaches, but totally unknown to the Anglos who claimed it. The territory was the Indians' hunting ground, their hiding place following raids into Mexico and through the widely scattered Anglo settlements along the lengthy frontier.

Col. Ranald S. Mackenzie was taking care of the Indians in the Texas Panhandle. The Battle of Palo Duro Canyon on September 28, 1874, during which Mackenzie and his 4th Cavalry surprised the hostiles and killed more than 1,000 horses, really ended the Indian wars in Texas. From then on it was the detailed work of mopping up pockets of resistance throughout the territory.

G.W. Arrington enlisted as a private in Company E of the Texas Rangers on September 1, 1875, with a monthly salary of $120. Company E, commanded by Captain Neal Coldwell, was organized on June 11, 1874, and when Coldwell later became commander of Company A, Arrington moved with him.

Arrington apparently tried to join the Rangers during April, 1875, but was turned down because of his indictment for murder in Alabama. He told Major Jones the story, and Jones urged him to return to Greensboro and straighten the matter out. Arrington knew his life wouldn't be worth a long trial in Alabama so he refused. He hired out as a scout for the Rangers instead, getting to enlist later.

Jones, a competent field general, kept his depleted, and much stretched out Rangers, in localities most liable to Indian depredations. "With an escort of thirty or forty men, I visited the companies in turn and scouted the entire frontier from the head of the Nueces to Red River about once a month, taking a different route each time as far as practicable. Also made several scouts out to the border of the plains," he wrote.

During its first six months of service, the Frontier Battalion knew of forty parties of Indians on the frontier, and had fourteen engagements with them, "besides giving chase to many that we could not overtake." During the next six months, the Rangers had four engagements and chased several other Indian parties, forcing them to abandon their stolen horses. Jones reported, "In first of May of this time there were eight parties of Indians in at one time. I caught one of the parties, killed five and wounded one. Chased three other parties and could have caught more of them, but my force was too small, having only four companies of thirty men each in the field at the time."

The chases continued. The Rangers, in most instances, met the Indians coming into their patrol areas or found the Indians' trails and followed them, preventing the hostiles from doing any mischief.

During fiscal year 1875, the Rangers killed 27 Indians, wounded 14 "beside ten or twelve more we have reason to believe were killed or wounded." They captured one, Little Bull, sending him to the penitentiary. They recovered a Mexican boy stolen three years prior on the Medina River west of San Antonio, and they recovered "about one hundred horses and two hundred cattle." The Rangers had two men killed, six wounded, 13 horses killed and nine wounded.

Jones reported to the Legislature that the Rangers "have rendered assistance to the civil authorities in maintaining law and suppression of crime a great many times, in several instances having been called to the interior counties for that purpose. Have broken up several organizations of outlaws and fugitives from justice. Have had six fights with them. Have arrested and turned over to the civil authorities about one hundred fugitives from justice and recovered from white thieves fifteen or twenty thousand dollars worth of cattle and horses and returned them to the rightful owner."

Because of his exceptional ability to scout and his extensive military background, Arrington was promoted to First Sergeant in 1876.

The frontier was moving slowly westward. Young, Clay, Shackleford, Eastland, Coleman, Kimble and Tom Green counties had been settled. McCulloch and Stephens Counties, organized early in 1876, were being formed and settled. Young County, organized in 1859, had a population of from a thousand to twelve hundred, but all had been driven to the interior by Indians 12—13 years prior, and it was only in 1876 that the people started resettling the county. Stephens, Palo Pinto, Coleman and parts of Parker and Jack counties also had been depopulated, but settlers were returning and asking for protection.

O.M. Keesay, a rancher near Fort Davis, expressed his fears to Louis Cardis, representative from the 75th District, in a letter dated June 8, 1876: "The Indians are bad. We have saved the herds four times in the last 40 days. They have taken away 21 head of animals and mortally wounded one of my best men. For God's sake, if you can do anything toward getting 25 stands of arms for us, do so. There is 18 men now in the mountains with old shotguns and all class of arms worthless."

On October 12, 1876, Rep. Cardis wrote to General William Steel at Austin: "Only a few days ago I forwarded a telegram to you informing you that recently in El Paso County, the Indians had killed two men and stolen and taken off a great many head of stock, requesting you to inform me whether El Paso and Presidio Counties were to have any protection and if so, when the protection would be given. On the 8th inst the Indians attacked three men employed of the Texas & California Stage Company at Eagle Spring station in El Paso Co., killing Chon Marujo and wounding Felipe Garcia and the Indians then moved upon the mail station intending to take the animals, but were repulsed by the efforts and resistance of the three men remaining at the corral. . . . On the 10th inst the Indians stole and carried off a herd of horses from the ranch of Miguel Monlaya in El Paso County and between the 15th and 24th ult the Indians carried off many heads of horses and cattle at various times from different persons, residents of El Paso County and within the same period killed the two men referred to in my telegram. . . . The people and property of El Paso and Presidio Counties are without protection and I consider it my duty as their representative to give you this information. I was within three miles of Montajas ranch on the 10th and arrived at Eagle Spring station 36 hours after the Indians killed Marujo."

And so it went. Outlaws, Indians, renegades of all types, and the settlers continued asking the Adjutant General and Governor for protection. With an active frontier, the Rangers were constantly on the move. Captain Coldwell, in his *Record of Scouts,* dated April 30, 1877, described the work Company A was doing:

"April 5th: Sergeant Arrington and 11 men left camp to arrest horses thieves near Pendencia, arrested Sam Williams found in possession of stolen property. Sent to jail at Eagle Pass. Also captured 11 oxen and five horses and turned them over to sheriff of Maverick Co., distance marched 225 miles. . . . Sergeant Arrington and 7 men left command and arrested Bill Allison, distance 27 miles. . . . Sergeant Arrington and 3 men arrested Roe Dublin, Wm Collins and Jack Hall. Distance 10 miles. . . . April 27th: Sergt Arrington and four men left camp to arrest Stark Reynolds, could not be found."

In a letter to Major Jones dated July 10, 1877, Capt. Coldwell wrote: "I returned from San Hollow-Black Creek and the country east of there on the 5th, Sgt. Arrington on the 6th and Sgt. Whelon on the 8th. We only caught three men that I wanted, but the capture of such a man as Wolfe has a better effect on the criminal class than the arrest of a dozen common men. He was regarded as one of the invincibles until we went after him. He is in the Castroville jail now."

Arrington quit the Rangers during September, 1877, but apparently his resignation was shortlived. Major Jones had decided to transfer Capt. Coldwell to command Company D and had planned to make Arrington a lieutenant and commander of Company A. When he learned of Arrington's resignation, he had no one suitable for the command post. Jones told Coldwell: "Having no one suitable to take command of Co. 'A' of course I could not take you away from it. Have not yet determined what I will do for a commander for Co. 'D', and will not until I come out. Worcester is recommended by a majority of the men in the company and by a few men in Kerr County. L.P. Sieker is recommended by a few of the men in the company and five petitions numerously signed by citizens of Kimble, Menard and Mason Counties, but as under the law neither citizens or enlisted men have a right to select an officer for the Company, I shall take my own time and manner to find someone who I believe to be sufficiently well qualified to justify me in recommending him to the Governor for appointment to the command of the Company."

Arrington, meanwhile, changed his mind and remained in the Rangers. On December 25, 1877, he was promoted to First Lieutenant and assigned to command Company C. In recommending Arrington's promotion, Jones wrote to Gen. William Steele: "Sergt Arrington has been in the service nearly three years, a greater part of the time under my personal observation. I have tested him thoroughly in the management of men, in commanding detachments & in his capacity for business & think him well qualified for this position. . . ."

His first job as commander of Company C was to arrest Alf Rushing, the murderer of the marshal in Freestone County. Sheriff J.P. Robinson of Wortham informed the Rangers that Rushing was in Navarro County "harbored about Mt. Pisgah and backed by some forty-five or fifty men." Jones told the sheriff he had no company to send that far into the interior, but that "Lt. Arrington is a discreet officer. He will investigate the situation and if he concludes that the arrest can be made by three or four men, I can send that number with him. Even in that event, I will have to ask the citizens to mount the men as they will have to go from here on the railroad."

Rushing eluded Arrington and his men.

Several months later, during August, 1878, Jones sent Arrington an anonymous letter he'd received stating that Rushing could be found near Cambridge. "Enclosed I hand you an anonymous letter in regard to Alf Rushing. I attach very little importance to such communications and seldom notice them, but as I am particularly desirous that Rushing should be caught I send you the letter and if you are not engaged in something very important, wish you to go to Cambridge and hunt up this secret service man. I will warn you, however, in advance that my experience teaches me that most of these secret service fellows are frauds and cheats of the most palpable character."

Whether Arrington contacted the secret service man or not wasn't recorded. Rushing wasn't found, and as far as can be determined, he never was captured by Arrington. With so many outlaws running loose, the Rangers hardly had time to devote tracking down any particular one anyway.

Arrington and nine men left camp for Erath and Comanche Counties to arrest the murderers of "old man Mackey and Jack McDonald" and when he arrived, he was joined by Sheriff Wilson and four deputies. Following an all night ride, the Rangers and county officers arrested 15 men.

They camped 20 miles east of Comanche and were settling down for the night when a party of 50 or 60 men armed with shotguns rode up.

"We've come to help you guard the prisoners," a spokesman said. Behind him could be heard, "Right." "We'll make sure they don't escape."

Arrington and his men spread out slowly, moving between the riders and the prisoners. "Just keep back," Arrington told them. "We don't need any help."

"Now, that's not very friendly. We just want to make sure they all make it to jail," the spokesman said.

Arrington wasn't one to fool around when he was outnumbered and outgunned. Turning to his nine men and the sheriff and his four deputies, he said, "Shoot the first man that comes any nearer." The Rangers cocked their rifles, pulled pistols from holsters and waited. None of the riders moved. Impasse. Suddenly the spokesman for the riders turned his horse around and rode through the bunched up horsemen.

"We'll be back!" one of them called out.

The law enforcement officers stayed alert until every rider was out of sight. Arrington posted guards and the men settled in for the night.

The camp was awake early. Preparations were made to take the prisoners into Comanche. Just then, however, 20 riders came loping over the hill.

"Hold it right there," Arrington gestured. Turning to his men, he told them to fall in, rifles ready. "You men turn around and go back into town. If you don't, we'll open fire."

There were no heroes among the riders. They turned their horses and rode out of sight. Arrington posted his men around the prisoners and rode alertly into town and put them in jail.

Arrington said later that he learned armed bodies of men were riding throughout Erath and Comanche Counties, "trying I suppose to intimidate the good citizens and witnesses. This is a mob numbering over 100 men and they are trying to rule that section, having sent numerous anonymous letters to parties not belonging to their mob. One of their party has divulged their secrets—giving all their pass words, signs, oath and everything connected with them—and the parties arrested are the ring leaders. Their trial will commence in a few days. Sheriff Wilson thinks he can manage to hold the prisoners, but if they are refused bail, I think he will lose them."

The fifteen prisoners were the sheriff's problem, however, and not Arrington's. He had other things to do. He learned that several bands of Indians were camped about 100 miles north of his Camp Loma Vista headquarters, and about 40 miles from settlements in Wilbarger County. The Indians had camped at the headwaters of Beaver Creek, and ranchers in the area were losing livestock. "The Indians were abusing every white man they found." Arrington contacted Major Jones and asked if he should make the trip. "I'm satisfied we can bring scalps back with us," he wrote. Jones telegraphed back, "You can make scout after Indians but be cautious."

Arrington left camp January 1, 1879 with 17 men and scouted northwest to the Brazos. One rancher told him that 10 Comanches were camped between the Brazos and Wichita rivers. However, a heavy snow storm, lasting several days, prevented him from tracking the Indians. When the storm subsided, Arrington and his men moved through the divide between the Pease and Wichita rivers, but had to return to their camp on the Mike O'Brien Ranch on the north prong of the Wichita because of more snow.

He was more successful on January 15. They spotted the trail of about 20 Indians, and saw them running in the distance. The chase began. Arrington's men killed one Indian, and while after the others, found a camp of 14 lodges and about 150 ponies on the

Pease River, five miles from where the Indian was shot. The Rangers charged the camp and cut the surprised Indians off from their horses. Then the Rangers got the surprise of their lives—among the Indians were several U.S. soldiers!

"They informed me that Sergt Jackson and nine men of the 10th U.S. Cavalry, stationed at Fort Sill, with 40 days rations, were ordered to bring 'Heap of Bears' band of Kiowa Indians to the Pease River to hunt. I went into their camp and found 18 warriors and about 20 squaws and children. The Indian killed belonged to this party and had in his possession a U.S. Springfield carbine loaned to him by Corporal Cox. . . . I returned the carbine to him, it being shot in the stock. The sergeant said they allowed the Indians to go 25 and 30 miles away. . . . Did not further molest the Indians and returned seven miles to our camp on the divide."

Arrington figured there were probably two thousand Indians "pretending that their mission was hunting" on Texas soil then, and he was of the opinion there would be an outbreak in the Spring of 1879. He subscribed to the frontiersman's belief that a good Indian was a dead one, and this was understandable. The Indians were in a struggle for survival, and they weren't giving up land they had roamed freely in for centuries without fighting for it. But the times were changing. The frontier was moving westward, Indians or no. The Texas Panhandle, once looked upon as uninhabitable by early explorers, Coronado among them, was being settled. The Indians, finding they couldn't cope with the constant flow of homesteaders and the increasing pressure from the Rangers and military, moved into Mexico, New Mexico and Arizona.

Fort Elliott, established February 3, 1875, was built to open the Texas Panhandle to settlement and to prevent the re-entry of Indians from Oklahoma Territory into West Texas.

Major James Biddle left Dodge City, Kansas, in December, 1874, with four companies of the Fourth Cavalry to select a site for the post. In January they camped near the Washita River, where they remained for three months, then moved to a new camp at Cantonment Creek in Gray County, Texas. Site for the fort was selected on May 18, 1875, near Sweetwater Creek in what was to become Wheeler County, Texas. Originally, the fort was a sub-post of Fort Sill and was known as Cantone Sweetwater or Cantonment, North Fork, Red River. It was named officially on February 21, 1876, after Major Joel H. Elliott, who was killed in the Battle of the Washita on November 29, 1868.

There never were many soldiers stationed there; usually less than 500. Part of the time several companies of the all-Negro Tenth Infantry made up the garrison, and at other times units of the Fourth Cavalry and Tenth Cavalry were stationed there.

Lt. Col. J.W. Davidson, commandant, and Arrington didn't see eye to eye on the Indian situation. In *The Texas Rangers,* the late historian, Walter Prescott Webb, wrote that "the practice of the federal government of permitting Indians to come to Texas was bitterly resented by the cattlemen and settlers. The inclination of the Texas Rangers to kill these Indians was displeasing to the government. The friction that developed led to a clash between Captain Arrington of the Rangers and Lieutenant-Colonel J.W. Davidson in June of 1879."

Arrington and 20 men had left Fort Griffin with 40 days' rations and had camped on Sweetwater Creek near Fort Elliott. Wheeler County had organized recently over the protests of Lee and Reynolds, the post traders, who wanted to keep all the business at the fort. The two had talked Col. Davidson into forbidding soldiers from trading in the nearby town of Sweetwater (later Mobeetie) and had told their own employees they would be fired if they traded in the new community.

One of the post's employees was something less than discreet in expressing an opinion concerning the role of the Cavalry and Rangers in the Panhandle, and brought the wrath of Arrington down on his head.

"One John Donnelly, a clerk in the Post Traders Store, has said in substance as follows—that you said you would fire upon me and my men or put us in irons if we fired upon or molested any Indians in the Panhandle," he wrote to Davidson. "This man Donnelly is the one whom you honored as a messenger to me on the day of my arrival here—and for that reason I think his talk should be noticed. I therefore desire to know whether or not Donnelly expressed your intentions and policy, not that I have any fears of you in the execution of the enterprise, but for the purpose of laying the matter before the Governor and the Legislature of Texas, which is now in session."

Donnelly started back pedaling, protesting the wording of Arrington's letter, and wrote one of his own to Davidson. It was witnessed by First Lieutenant Charles L. Cooper, 10th Cavalry, Post Adjutant.

"The within statement as made by Capt. Arrington is not true. I said that if they did fire or kill an Indian that the Commanding Officer at Fort Elliott should fire on them and put them in irons. I further said that the only object in getting these Rangers here was to provoke an Indian war."

Arrington answered that ridiculous charge in a letter to the Adjutant General on June 21, 1879:

"I understand that the Sutler is getting up a petition to send to

Austin to have us removed from the Panhandle country, and if so, it will be signed by their employees and three of the county commissioners whom they have under their control. If they do send it down, I would be pleased to have a copy. What their object is I cannot say, as we have not interferred in any way, shape or form with them or anyone else. They say we will bring on an Indian war as I intend to kill the first Indian I see, I am just informed. The Co. Atty. heard my conversation with Col. Davidson and I did not say that my orders were to kill the first Indian I saw, but were to give protection to life and property whether against Indians or white men. That if I found Indians coming into the State with arms, and in sections where they were depredating, that I would certainly go farther. . . ."

For all the smoke raised by the sutler and his employees, nothing came of their efforts to remove the Rangers. The incident did, however, add to Arrington's reputation as a tough, hardnosed Ranger willing to take on the U.S. Army if need be.

Col. Charles Goodnight, cattleman and former Ranger scout, might have had something to say about it if they had been successful in ridding the area of Arrington and his men.

Goodnight, who brought one of the first cowherds into the Texas Panhandle's Palo Duro Canyon in 1876, had been losing too many cattle to marauding Indians and he was fed up with it. He told Arrington so during one of Arrington's stops at the Goodnight Ranch. The time was July, 1879. Arrington reported to headquarters that "this is a large ranch, and lost very heavy last winter to Indians, and Goodnight told me that he was not going to stand it any longer, and that if he did not get some protection he would go to fighting the Indians himself." Goodnight had had his share of Indian fighting in past years, and he told Arrington he could raise 75 well armed men anytime.

"If you need the extra men, just ask."

Arrington observed that "Indians are in the Panhandle country all the time camping around, apparently friendly, but for the purpose of killing stock.

1879 apparently was a year of transition in the Plains country. There was considerable activity among Indians, outlaws and settlers. The Indians wanted to keep what had been theirs. The outlaws wanted to take what belonged to the Indians and the settlers. And the settlers wanted peace and quiet to farm and raise their families.

The Rangers riding through Briscoe and Floyd Counties observed that "stock ranches are as thick as they can be on all the streams that head along the Plains. There are settlers and emi-

26

G.W. (CAP) ARRINGTON.

grants coming in every day and everyone seems to be uneasy about Indians and white thieves." Arrington found Blanco Canyon in Crosby County to be a regular path way for both Indians and outlaws, and that "not a week passes but what horse thieves pass out, taking the trail from the head of the Canyon to Fort Stanton and the Pecos, 150 miles away."

White men moved in bands of six to fifteen and Indians prowled in groups of ten to seventy-five and sometimes more. Arrington, feeling that a company of Rangers would be strong enough to stop the roving outlaws and Indians, established Camp Roberts in Crosby County as headquarters for Company C on September 9, 1879. He moved from his camp near Fort Griffin in Shackelford County to the new station near the mouth of Blanco Canyon to patrol an area including the Pecos River west into New Mexico, a distance of about 300 miles, and extending from the Canadian River to the north to the headwaters of the Devil River to the south, a distance of 500 miles, "an unknown country to white men and without a single white inhabitant."

The story of Arrington's discovery of the location of the rumored "Lost Lakes" is what legends are made of. The Lakes, thought to be in the Sand Hill country of West Texas or eastern New Mexico, were the jumping off point for many raids by both Comanches and Apaches. The Lakes were, as it turned out, the final refuge for Indians on the run from raids into the settled areas along the westward-moving frontier. Arrington knew that by finding where the Indians headed following their raids he could eliminate the hiding place as an area of safety in the uncharted desert country, and that is what he set out to do when he learned of a raid on the Slaughter Ranch, 20 miles south of his headquarters, on December 28, 1879.

During that winter a band of hostile Apaches had been coming from some point in this unknown region and raiding stock ranches along the west edge of the Texas Plains, stealing horses primarily. Arrington's principal mission at that time was to break up the raids and follow and discover, if possible, the hiding place of the Indians.

About noon of that December day, two cowboys from the Slaughter Ranch reported to Arrington that on the previous night Indians had driven off a large number of horses. "Within two hours after receiving this information, twelve of my men, including myself, with 10 days' rations and other equipment loaded on pack mules, were in our saddles and hurrying to the Slaughter Ranch to take up the trail. . . ." Thus began one of the most spectacular scouts ever made into unknown territory.

Included among the Rangers were Arrington, Sergeant Dick Jones, Corporal Joe Rush, John D. Birdell, P.S. Bell, John Dunn, J.B. Gibson, Harney Hamner, Hiram McMurray, William Stonebreaker, Will Snearly, James McElroy and a Ranger named Callihan.

They reached the ranch and picked up the trail about 5 o'clock that same evening. The trail led south, passing the mouth of Yellowhouse Canyon, where it climbed the rimrock onto the Plains proper and turned west. As night was falling, they made camp. A misty rain began to come down, and by morning everything was covered with a shield of ice.

"We again took up the trail, following it west by Tahoka Lake, thence to Double Lakes, a distance of about 30 miles, where night again overtook us and we camped. The following morning I discovered that the trail led off directly west from Double Lakes and into a country that was, at that time, utterly unknown to white man."

Arrington hesitated, recalling what he knew about Captain Nicholas Nolan's adventures with the 10th U.S. Cavalry a few years back in that same area. "Nolan followed a band of Indians from some point east of the Staked Plains over this same route." However, Nolan's scout into the area became a disaster.

Capt. Nolan, Arrington recalled, in compliance with Special Order No. 104, from Headquarters Fort Concho, Tex., July 3, 1877, left the fort at 9 a.m., July 10, and marched up the North Concho River a distance of 20 miles before setting up camp.

On the 11th, he scouted an additional 25 miles up the North Concho to a point known as Camp Hudson. "This day," Nolan reported, "one man was sun struck but soon recovered from the effect."

Nolan continued up the North Concho, finally leaving it to follow a trail leading to Big Spring. On July 14, he marched to Wild Horse Springs east of Big Spring, and on the 15th, scouted to the Colorado River. Two days later he came across 28 men camped 7 miles northeast of the Muchaque Mountains. "They were following and recovering stock stolen by Indians. They had with them a guide, a Mexican by the name of Jose Anaya who had an extensive knowledge of the Staked Plains, and who had formerly been a Guide with General Mackenzie. . . . The party requested me to accompany them in their search for Indians, and having no Guide with my Command I was only too happy to accede to their request. . . ."

The group prepared for a 20 days scout, and on July 19, Nolan, First Lt. C.S. Cooper, 40 enlisted men and 22 civilians left camp. They marched to the main prong of the Colorado River, 15 miles away, and camped.

"July 21st, 1877. At 7 O'clock A.M. left camp and marched 8 miles to a point on Tobacco Creek, where we halted, were deciding to make a night march to Laguna Sabinas. At about 4 o'clock P.M. Quimia, a Quohada Chief of the Comanche tribe came into my camp and produced a pass from the Indian agent at Fort Sill, I.T., dated July 12, 1877, which was countersigned by Colonel R.S. Mackenzie, 4th Cavalry, commanding Fort Sill. The pass authorized him and party to be absent from the reservation forty days; the purport of the pass seemed to indicate that they were on a mission for the purpose of inducing and to bring back Indians that had left the reservations; being perfectly satisfied that the pass was genuine, and finding that he and party were liberally supplied with Government horses, Equipments, Arms, Ammunition and Rations, I did not feel authorized in detaining him."

Nolan and his party proceeded to Laguna Sabinas, a distance of 50 miles, arriving there at 8 a.m., July 22. Water for the entire command was becoming critical, and Nolan was compelled to "dig several holes and dip out the water with small tin cups, and securing it in camp kettles, in order to obtain enough for men and animals."

The Comanches visited Nolan's camp again on the 23rd. The exact spelling of the Comanche chief leading the Indians apparently was beyond his understanding. This time he called the chief "Quania the Quohada Chief." It is possible he was dealing with Quanah Parker.

Water was becoming increasingly difficult to find. Jose Anaya was unable to locate any, and Nolan started back toward Double Lakes. Upon arrival he had the same difficulties in obtaining water he had at Laguna Sabinas, a cupful at a time from deep holes.

Then, on July 26, 1877, Anaya spotted the tracks of forty Indians heading northeast, and Nolan and his command started after them. They marched to Dry Lake, arriving there just prior to sundown. "I here found the Guide and balance of his party. At this place no water could be found either for men or horses. I then asked Jose how far it was to water. He told me 15 or not more than 20 miles. I then continued on in a direct westerly course to strike the trail. . . ."

Darkness forced them to camp. The next morning Nolan started out again, following the trail until mid-afternoon "at which time was compelled to abandon it on account of the ponies of the Guide and citizens giving out." He was in the vicinity of the Sand Hills. The scout had followed the trail of the Indians for 25 miles. The Indians scattered to confuse their trackers, but the main trail was located again. The entire command was beginning to suffer for water. "One of my men . . . fell from his horse from the effect of sun stroke. I then asked the Guide how far it was to water, he replied 6 or 7 miles. . . ."

Anaya was given a fresh horse to hunt for water. The command, now suffering greatly, followed his trail as best they could. They followed Anaya for 15 miles. Several of the recruits gave out, continually falling from their horses. More men became ill with sunstroke. "Owing now to the exhausted condition of the men I was compelled to halt for a while and fully expected that the Guide had found water and would soon join us. . . ." Nolan had sent eight men on ahead with canteens, instructing them to return as soon as they found water. "Up to this time we had marched about 50 miles under a broiling sun over a barren sandy plain without a drop of water—from statements of the Guide I had fully expected to have found water during the early part of the day. I did not again see the eight men . . . until my arrival at the supply camp on August 6th."

The command was in a bad way now. Nolan assigned Sergeant William L. Umbles to remain with two sick men with instructions to bring them into camp as soon as they were able. "This sergeant instead of doing as directed . . . came up and passed on by the camp within easy hailing distance without halting, although challenged by myself, and one of the command who had been sent back to show them into camp, thereby cowardly and disgracefully deserting the command."

The sergeant's wasn't the only desertion. Nolan, convinced now that his Guide was lost, felt his only hope was to get to Double Lakes. His men were completely exhausted, "continually falling from their horses. . . ." One man fainted and Nolan told a corporal and another man to remain with the stricken soldier. "This Corporal instead of obeying my orders by rejoining the Command as soon as the man was able, most disgracefully deserted the sick man and the man left with him. . . . Soon after this, Half Lance Corporal Fremont without any authority together with two men took their horses and two pack mules and deserted the Command, which was at this time suffering intensely for want of water."

They finally killed a horse, distributing its blood among the men. The remainder of the command finally reached Double Lakes after having been without water for 86 hours. Some of the deserters never were found.

Arrington, in recalling the incident, remarked that "this was the last expedition of any kind whatsoever that even attempted to enter this unknown country up to the time that I went in there." He didn't make the mistake Nolan did. "Instead of following the

Indian trail as it led west from Double Lakes and into the desert as Capt. Nolan had done, I sent one of the men, John D. Birdell, back to my headquarters for a wagon and additional supplies and some empty water kegs, with orders to wait at Double Lakes until our arrival. . . . We turned northwest and after two days march reached what is known as the Yellow Houses, a point on the old trail running west from the headwaters of the Brazos across the plains to old Fort Sumner on the Pecos River in New Mexico. This point was about 50 miles west of my headquarters in Blanco Canyon."

George and John Causey, buffalo hunters, had a winter camp three miles north of the Yellow Houses, a bluff some 160 feet high. The caves in the bluff gave it its name. The Causey Brothers established their camp there during the winter of 1879-80.

Arrington stopped by the camp and bought two fresh buffalo hides from the hunters and fashioned them into a "kind of saddle bag and fitted them onto a couple of pack saddles. In each end of these bags we fitted a 10-gallon water keg. We then filled the four kegs with water from the spring, strapped them on the pack mules, and leaving the wagon and everything else that we could not take along . . . we broke camp and followed the old trail west about 10 miles to Silver Lake, where we camped for the night."

The nights were bitter cold, and the springs at Silver Lake froze. Arrington and his men broke through the ice so their horses could drink. Arrington's plan was to make a two days' march from Silver Lake toward the southwest into the desert to intersect the Indian trail he had left at Double Lakes. He believed that by riding 12 hours a day he could travel from 80 to 100 miles, and if he failed to find water within that time, he would fill the canteens from the four water kegs, give the remainder to the horses and retrace his route.

At sunrise, they fell into line and, taking their course by a small pocket compass, they started at a brisk walk into the unknown region. For the first few miles, they rode on dark sand covered with a heavy turf of grass, then onto a reddish loose sand with scattered vegetation. At the end of about 30 miles march, they came in sight of the real desert "absolutely barren of vegetation, almost white as snow; certainly by far the most desolate and uninviting region that I ever beheld," Arrington recalled.

He knew the reputation of the region for "bewildering the brain, choking the throat, parching the lips and swelling the tongue of man and beast, even unto death." Even so, they approached it, plunged into it and traveled on and on. They had to slow down because their horses, at every step, sank almost halfway to their knees in the loose white sands. They camped that night "in one of the wildest and most desolate spots imaginable." When it was light enough to see the needle of the compass, they began their march again.

The sun came up and climbed higher and higher, casting its glistening rays down upon the white sands. Mirages formed. Miles away a lake, bordered by groves of trees, appeared. "It was so natural that one could scarcely believe they were not real." The scene shifted, changed, disappeared and another took its place in another direction. "While looking at these strange phantoms, it was easy to understand why one, half crazed with the heat and thirst, as were those dusky troopers of the 10th U.S. Cavalry, would run with all remaining strength trying to reach these imaginary lakes only to find nothing there and finally to fall exhausted and perish amid the desolation."

All day long they held to their course, never varying, "with only the billowing white sand extending in a limitless distance in every direction, the whole pervaded by an awful silence—a silence that you could almost hear." Late that afternoon the appearance of the country changed. They rode out of the sand hills into level ground. The earth was more solid and some vegetation grew.

They crossed an old cavalry trail, two narrow trails running parallel 20 feet apart. The Rangers followed the trail a short distance. "Nolan's, no doubt," Arrington surmised. The cavalry trail, then two years old, moved away from Arrington's intended route, and the men turned back. Directly in front of them, three to four miles away, was a low hill. They reached the hill just as the sun was sinking beneath the western horizon.

"Will you look at that!" one exclaimed.

Looking down they saw a dry salt lake along the western base of the hill.

"Well, that's no mirage anyway," one observed.

Arrington scanned the lake and its surroundings with his field glasses.

"Nothing," he said.

They moved forward slowly, passing around the north end of the lake to the west side, where they found several springs of brackish water. Enough light remained for them to discover that a large band of horses had been driven in recently and watered.

Several fires had been kindled and four to five horses had been killed, with "every particle of flesh cut from their frames." The Indian sign was fresh.

"Hey, look what I've found," one called out, pointing to a huge shoulder blade of a buffalo. "An Indian sign board."

The bone was one of the largest any of the Rangers had ever seen and had been exposed to the hot desert sun for many years. It

33

was bleached white as snow. The fan-shaped bone was 14-16 inches long, 10 inches wide at one end, tapering to two inches in diameter at the other. One side was perfectly smooth.

Holding the ancient sign board up, Arrington and his men saw two lines of large shod horse tracks running parallel and in the direction of the opposite side of the board. In front of the tracks was an Indian leading a pony with tepee poles lashed to his sides and dragging on the ground behind him. Resting upon the poles was baggage. In front of the Indian and near the left hand edge of the board were some Indian tepees, some trees and an Indian standing near a fire apparently cooking.

"They know we're following them," Arrington said. "They've moved their camp farther west to some point they believe is safe. They left the board here to tell any friends who might come in after them."

The Rangers camped at the lake that night and christened it Ranger Lake. The next morning they scouted the area and noted that several bands of horses had been driven in for water recently. They also located a large trail leading off toward the southwest. There were marks of tepee poles along the trail. They broke camp and followed the trail for nearly 20 miles, and saw a chain of four small lakes running along the base of a hill and extending northwest and southwest. Each of the lakes was about a fourth of a mile in length and separated by a narrow neck of land. A valley extended out from the lakes, ending at a large bluff. The Rangers skirted around the west side and found several springs of brackish water. They also found considerable Indian sign, camp fires and skeletons of several recently killed horses. All the meat had been stripped from the bones.

"Ashes are still warm," one of the Rangers said. "We're getting close."

A fresh trail led off toward the southwest. Arrington, never one to make hasty decisions, called his Rangers around him, and although none needed reminding, he said, "We're in hostile Indian country so stay alert. There are at least 250 miles of desert and plains country between us and our headquarters. The Indians know this country. We don't. And something else. Supplies are running short and our horses are pretty weak. If we had to run for it, we could be in trouble." The men nodded their acknowledgement of that. "One more thing. From the course and the rate we've traveled, we're far beyond the boundary of Texas. In other words, we're out of our jurisdiction, and that might become a problem if we did come upon the Indians. As much as I don't like it, we'll stop here and return to Ranger Lake in the morning."

Arrington knew that the Indians made raids on settlers on

moonlit nights and that the lake appeared to be the first watering place after crossing the desert. "There's a chance Indians may be on their way out of the Plains. We'll stop at the lake until after the full moon. Maybe we can intercept them."

They set up camp in a low range of sand hills on the west side of Ranger Lake, concealing themselves and horses as best they could. Rations were cut to less than a half ration per day per man. Pickets were put out south and west on the high ground, each with strong field glasses. "Keep a close lookout, especially toward the east. If they're coming in, it'll be from that direction," Arrington said.

The Rangers stayed at the lake for 15 days. The days were clear and warm. The nights were bitter cold. Their rations consisted of bacon, flour and coffee without sugar. The supply of bacon ran out. The horses had practically nothing to eat, and Arrington observed that "our stay here was simply gradual starvation for both men and horses." Game was plentiful, but under the circumstances the Rangers didn't want to use up their ammunition shooting antelope.

Arrington finally sent Joe Rush, R.S. Bell and J.B. Gibson back to the four lakes to kill some antelope. They returned the following day and reported they had seen 20 Indians at the lakes.

"They spotted us, and tried to get our horses," Bell said. "From the Indian sign around the lakes, there's a large body of Redskins near."

Arrington, looking around at his command, decided not to return to the four lakes. The odds were against them. Their numbers were small. The horses were weak and they were a long ways from headquarters On January 31, 1880, they broke camp and started toward home.

The trek back was a nightmare. The first day on the homeward journey was bright and clear. The men killed an antelope and ate every particle of it for supper. The next morning, however, it began to snow and by daylight the ground was covered. Arrington, in recalling that day, said, "The snow was coming from the northeast. It would be hard to imagine a more forlorn aspect than the little squad of men and horses presented that morning as they fell in line and took up the march facing that terrible blizzard half famished with not a morsel of food, the horses almost exhausted reeled as they walked, the men gaunt and haggard from starvation, their faces drawn and pinched until their most intimate friends would not have recognized them."

They plodded on. None had ever experienced such bone-freezing cold. No one spoke. Their misery was evident.

Arrington knew that 50 to 60 miles northeast there were the

caves of the Yellowhouses and the Causey Brothers' buffalo camp. "There was relief if we could but reach these points. But I also knew that if we should miss them, there was little chance for us in that terrible storm."

They marched all day long. For 18 hours they faced "that awful snow storm" with the mercury at 10 below zero. "Those who know anything about a blizzard on the north plains of Texas may have some idea of our situation." Night came and there was no relief in sight. The snow had reached a depth of 12 to 14 inches.

John Birdwell was the first to give up. "I can't go on," he cried. "My horse has given out." His hands and feet were paralyzed with cold.

Arrington halted the men and had them bring up an old Indian pony they had caught at Ranger Lake. They put Birdwell on him and tied him on with a rope. They moved forward again, each movement agony beyond description. They were covered from head to foot with a shield of ice.

Then, miracle of miracles, it stopped snowing and the clouds started to break up. A star appeared, as welcome as water in the desert. Using the star as their guide, the found, after a 30 minute march, the Yellowhouses and the place where they had left their wagon on the way out. They found shelter for themselves and their horses. About a hundred feet from their wagon they found a cave large enough to shelter the whole squad. A fire of mesquite wood was started. The thawing out process began.

First, they cut Birdwell's gloves and boots off and carried him into the cave and laid him near the fire. "He was suffering so with cold that he rolled over and passed his hands through the fire." The pain! Birdwell passed out, and the men dragged him out into the snow to rub his feet and hands. The Ranger came to, and was taken back into the cave. He tried to shove his hands back into the warmth of the fire. Again the men dragged him outside to rub snow on his frozen hands and feet. Then they returned him to the cave and piled blankets on top of him and placed a guard on him to keep him away from the fire.

The men settled down for the night, warming themselves as best they could by the fire. The next morning Arrington sent two men with pack mules to the Causey camp. They brought back several hundred pounds of buffalo meat, flour, sugar and other supplies. Rations were issued out sparingly. "The men were so weak from hunger and exposure to cold that they could scarcely stand up, and some of them, when attempting to walk, would turn blind."

They rested and ate and ate and rested. A couple of days later they continued their march toward their headquarters, reaching camp three days later. The men had been away for 40 days.

Arrington, in writing his report of the adventure, said, "We had been given up as lost. On this trip we had traveled between five and six hundred miles in the dead of winter on less than half rations for ourselves and almost nothing for our horses.

"In my opinion, few men have suffered more and lived than did this little squad of Rangers during the campaign. . . . Certainly no men are more deserving of honor and reward. . . . Their services in this campaign were invaluable in that they penetrated a region of country that was at the time absolutely unknown to white men and discovered lakes of water in the heart of the Great Desert. They also discovered the hiding place of this band of hostile Indians which had been raiding the frontier of Texas from time immemorial and broke up their rendezvous. They were never known to make a raid on that part of the Frontier of Texas again."

Arrington's report prompted Lt. Col. John T. Hatch, 4th Cavalry, Brevet Brigadier General, USA, commander at Fort Sill, Indian Territory, to write on February 10, 1880: "I see in a paper that Lieut. Arrington has visited a lake on the Staked Plains near the boundary of New Mexico. This lake is supposed to be one never before visited by white men. We have known for some time that there was such a lake, but the great distance from this post has prevented our sending a force to locate it. The lake was not known to the Comanches until Mackenzie's campaign against them in 1872, when the Apaches informed them of its existence. It is claimed by the Indians that it can only be reached by a march of two days without water.

"You will confer a great favor if you will furnish me a description of the route taken by Lieut. Arrington in going to it, and if he returned by another route, a description of that also. It is from the point referred to that most or all of the raids on western Texas in the past year have started. The actors in these raids have been Apaches with a few Comanches who ran away from this reserve last spring."

A copy of Arrington's report was sent, and Hatch replied, "In conversation with Indians belonging to the Quaha-die (sic) Comanches, who formerly made the lakes described by the Captain as a place of refuge, I learn that they are what is known to rumor as the 'Lost Lakes.'

"I enclose with this a copy of a letter received today from Colonel Hunt, agent for the Kiowas and Comanches. I do not place much confidence in the report as to the number of arms sold, but do believe that Doan habitually sells both arms and ammunition to the Indians of this reservation in violation of the laws of Texas. There is a belief no United States law forbids such sales within the limits of any state, for which reason I call your attention to the letter of the Agent."

Doan's Store, founded by Judge Jonathan Doan in 1875, was approximately 15 miles north of present-day Vernon, Texas, on the Red River. Many historians have stated the Judge C.F. Doan and his nephew, Corwin Doan, operated Doan's Store. However, Terry A. Wheatley of Amarillo, a grandson of Judge Doan, said the information is incorrect. "Judge Jonathan Doan and his nephew, Corwin F. Doan, operated the store. Judge Jonathan Doan, the first county judge of Wilbarger County, was my grandfather, my mother, Emma Doan Wheatley, being his daughter. Corwin F. Doan was the son of Azariah W. Doan and Judge Jonathan and Azariah were brothers. Judge Doan had no middle name. He had a son, also named Corwin Thomas (Major) Doan, who passed away on February 14, 1953, in Amarillo. Judge Doan previously had stores at Hays, Kansas; Fort Sill, Oklahoma, and on Buck Creek near Memphis, Texas, before establishing Doan's Store at Doan's Crossing on the Red River in 1875."

Arrington knew the Doans. He also knew that they knew Quanah Parker, the Comanche chief. While Arrington often accused the Doans of selling guns to the Indians, he never caught them in the act.

Doan's Crossing was regarded as the best jumping-off place for cattle drives to the northwest, and the Doans became prosperous selling supplies, whiskey, ammunition, guns, saddles, bridles, blankets to the men starting out on the long and adventurous northern trek. The crossing on the Western Trail was known throughout Texas and points north. Just how many cattle went up the Western Trail from south of Bandera, Texas to connect with the Bozeman Trail west of Ogallala, Nebraska, isn't known positively. More than 12 million horses and cattle went to northern markets during the trail-driving period. Six million of them are said to have crossed the Red River at Doan's Crossing.

BIBLIOGRAPHY

Chapter Two

Adjutant General's Office, various files, Austin, Texas

Arrington Papers given to Author by the late French Arrington, Canadian, Texas

Lone Star, A History of Texas and the Texans, T.R. Fehrenbach, The Macmillan Company, New York.

The Texas Rangers, Walter Prescott Webb, University of Texas Press, Austin, Texas.

Texas Rangers Papers, University of Texas Archives, Austin, Texas.

Earl Vandale Papers, ca. 1819-ca. 1947, University of Texas Archives, Austin, Texas.

Walter Prescott Webb Papers, University of Texas Archives, Austin, Texas. Terry A. Wheatley, 1615 Polk St., Amarillo, Tex., interview concerning Doan's Store and Doan's Crossing.

CAP ARRINGTON and his favorite horse, Jeff Davis.

CAP ARRINGTON, right, and his son, French (note he was on crutches then) check some of the hogs Arrington raised on his ranch near Candian, Tex.

CHAPTER THREE

Cowboys and Indians

At the end of 1879, the Frontier Battalion was down to five companies of 120 officers and men. Adjutant General John B. Jones had stationed the companies in counties where they could do the most good quickly.

Company A, Captain George W. Baylor, El Paso County
Company B, Captain Bryan Marsh, Mitchell County
Company C, Captain G.W. Arrington, Crosby County
Company D, Captain D.W. Roberts, Menard County
Company E, Lieutenant C.L. Nevill, Presidio County

Ten men were in Motley County and four men were in Austin.

During the years 1879 and 1880, the Frontier Battalion and a special force for the suppression of lawlessness and crime performed 1,001 scouts, had seven fights with Indians, followed 21 Indian trails, had five fights with outlaws, killed 12 outlaws and wounded four, arrested 685 fugitives from justice, attended 67 courts by request of civil authorities, furnished 67 jail and other guards, provided 180 escorts, recovered 1,917 horses and cattle and returned one Mexican child to his parents.

Captain Baylor's company at El Paso protected settlements against raids by Indians from the Fort Stanton Reservation in New Mexico and against lawless white men who infested the county.

His company also joined General Grierson of the United States Army in the operations against Victorio's band of Indians, a campaign that lasted three months, August, September and October, 1879. Adjutant General Jones wrote of Baylor's company:

"Again, in October, Capt. Baylor took the field against this notorious Indian chief—this time by invitation of the local Mexican authorities on the other side of the river, and scouted with General Terrassas of the Mexican forces some 20 days, when a few days before Victorio was overtaken, information was received from the central government of Mexico that the presence of foreign troops on Mexican soil could not be tolerated, and he, as well as the United States troops under General Buel, were requested to leave the country, which, of course, they did."

El Paso city officials wanted help from the Texas Rangers. The community, they said, was "over-run and over-awed by gamblers, rowdies, thieves and murderers," congregating there in anticipation of a rich harvest as soon as the Texas Pacific and Southern Pacific railroads reached the growing city. The El Paso mayor wanted the Rangers to "protect them against these lawless characters." Company A moved from Ysleta to El Paso.

Meanwhile, Company D, under Capt. Roberts, was sent in pursuit of a band of robbers hitting the merchants at Fort Davis. These daylight robberies were made by a gang led by Jesse Evans, said to be the "most daring outlaw of New Mexico." Troops stationed at Fort Davis, incidentally, played a major role in the campaigns against Victorio, whose death in 1880 terminated Indian warfare in Texas.

In his annual report to the Texas Legislature, Jones said of the daylight robberies: "I dispatched a detachment of Company D from Menard County to Fort Davis by forced marches. A few days after arriving there, they ascertained the whereabouts of the robbers, followed them forty or fifty miles toward the Mexican border, when a sharp fight ensued, resulting in killing one of the robbers, wounding one and capturing the rest of the party. One of the Rangers, Geo. R. Bingham of Company D, a gallant young fellow and good soldier, was killed by the outlaws in this affair."

Elsewhere, the three companies stationed on the border of the settled counties under Captains Roberts, Marsh and Arrington were continuing their scouts after Indians and outlaws. The field of their operations included the whole line of the frontier extending from Dimmitt County on the Nueces River to Fort Elliott in the Texas Panhandle, a distance of 500 miles, and as far west as Fort Stockton and the New Mexico line.

Baylor County, named for Texas Ranger surgeon H.W. Baylor, was created from Fannin County in 1879, with Seymour as the county seat.

The county courts and local law officers were unable to put down the lawlessness rampant in that section of the state, and Jones ordered Arrington, with a small detachment of his company, to help out. The Rangers remained in the county for two months, returned to their camp in Crosby County, but had to go back to Seymour during the early months of 1880. On April 9, Arrington wrote in his report to Jones:

"I left camp on 28 Mar and arrived at this place (Seymour) on 3rd inst. I find everything very quiet, owing, I suppose, to the want of whiskey—but a new supply is expected soon. I am informed by reliable parties that the difficulty between Constable Homer and the cowboy Wilson was the outcropping of an old feud and just at that time the Co. Atty. Thurmond made threats he intended to put the cowboys in irons when he got Rangers here and many other indiscreet remarks which made the boys mad and they shot and disturbed the peace more to spite the Constable and Co. Atty. than anything else—and too, knowing that the Sheriff was entirely inefficient. I have only seen one bullet hole in a house and do not think the cowboys intended any harm. There will be at least 150 men here in a few days to have a general roundup and if the whiskey arrives in time, I expect times will be lively, but after that I do not think there will be any more disturbance here than in other frontier towns situated in the center of a large cattle range."

The whiskey arrived, and on April 17, Arrington wrote that "the saloon opened several days ago and we have assisted in arresting four men charged with misdemeanor offenses. There was a shooting in the saloon this evening between two men—Henry Coveth, a cowman of Wichita and a man named Jim Milroy—both men are seriously, if not mortally, wounded. I think our presence and assistance have prevented other bloodshed. The cowboys are making a great many threats, but I think it is all talk."

Arrington wasn't too kind in his remarks concerning Seymour. On stationery from the office of Frank E. Conrad, a wholesale and retail dealer of staple dry goods, groceries (drovers' outfitting a specialty), at Fort Griffin, Arrington wrote:

"The roundups have passed and everything is quiet, but I am satisfied that trouble will occur as soon as we leave Seymour. The citizens of Seymour are about the contrariest set I have ever met. Each man pulls against his neighbor and no one takes any interest in the town or its officers—expecting us to do everything. The fellow Homer is still constable and as all the cow men are down on him, he, of course, is a standing menace to this country. I have advised his removal but no action has been taken. The sheriff has proven himself to be no account and the cowboys openly boast they will renew their disturbances. There are several leading men in Seymour who wink at all the shooting and one of them said he intended to make things hot after we left. . . . I made about 10 arrests at Seymour—misdemeanors—I do not think that courts can be held at Seymour provided any of the cowboys were to be tried. I think the old thing would occur again. They asked to crowd the court room armed with their guns and the officers were afraid to convict. Baylor is a good county and will soon settle up with some assistance. Seymour is improving or was until this trouble. There are 6 or 7 large store buildings going up and I think it will make a good town if quiet can be restored."

Arrington left six men in Seymour and took the remainder of his company on a scout for Indians to the southwest. Several parties of Indians had been spotted, and he thought he could catch them "at those lakes in the sand hills."

Seymour, meanwhile, settled down to an uneasy peace with the small detachment of Rangers there, but Arrington reported that "the people are growling among themselves and fighting occasionally. The boys arrested Judge Morris on a charge of assist to murder a few days before they left."

Arrington's disgust with Seymour was evident in his June 22, 1880, report to Jones. "There has been more trouble at Seymour. The people of Seymour are about the easiest set of men to bull doze I have ever met. One man can go into a crowd of 20 of them and do everything he pleases and no resentment will be offered. Judge Morris was disliked by all parties. The citizens of the town had no use for him and he never associated with the citizens, kept himself entirely isolated from them. I am satisfied that prominent married men have been and are now winking at all these disturbances."

Arrington was in Seymour various times during 1880, but despite small flare-ups among cowboys and businessmen, the town settled down as most frontier towns eventually did. Things were happening elsewhere, and Arrington and his men were moved about the Panhandle to handle them.

Major Jones died during July, 1881, and M.H. King was appointed to succeed him by Gov. Oran M. Roberts.

Walter Prescott Webb in *The Texas Rangers* wrote: "In reality the Frontier Battalion should have been disbanded with the death of Major Jones, not because of his death, but because the frontier was gone. Though the organization continued for twenty years longer, it did not operate as a frontier force."

Once the threat of the Comanches and Kiowas was removed, the Texas Panhandle opened to settlement. The Adobe Walls fight of June 27, 1874, had kept the buffalo hunters out of the Panhandle for several months, but by 1877 they had pretty well destroyed the big herds that had once roamed the Plains. Cattlemen started moving cattle into the Panhandle in 1876, and the big ranches of the 1880s and 1890s became a reality.

Arrington's company worked farther and farther north toward Mobeetie, the Mother City of the Panhandle, and Clarendon, dubbed Saints' Roost by hard-drinking cowboys, and Tascosa and Fort Elliott.

Indians from the Fort Sill Reservation in Oklahoma Territory came into the Panhandle to trade and to hunt the few remaining buffalo. Mostly the Indians crossed the Red River to trade at Doans near present day Vernon. Among the Indians was Quanah Parker, son of Cynthia Ann Parker. "I could have very easily rounded them up," Arrington wrote, "but owing to the reports of uneasiness among the Kiowas and Comanches, I thought it best to wait instructions. I can arrest Indians there almost any day. . . . They are very quiet and only want to trade."

Arrington was concerned that the Indians were buying guns

and ammunition from Judge Doan and his nephew, Corwin F. Doan. "I understand that Doan was indicted five times in Clay County Court for trading with the Indians, but gets out of it as the law forbids trading with hostile Indians. When Indians come over on this side to trade they are not considered hostile but friendly. . . ."

Cowboys and Indians. Although the Panhandle was filling with people, the citizens wanted more law enforcement than they were getting and asked that Rangers patrol the area more often. Clarendon residents asked that a squad be stationed in their town. Charles Goodnight, the Panhandle's Number One cattleman, and other leading stockmen, were "opposed to the rowdy cowboys," and wanted law and order brought to the community. Arrington, however, was of the opinion that "they can check it without our aid."

Saints' Roost wasn't always that saintly, although the Reverend Lewis Henry Carhart, the colony's founder, emphasized in his promotion literature that there would be "no whiskey forever" in the town. Once, when a whiskey peddler pulled his barrel-loaded wagon into town, Goodnight, Clarendon's unofficial protector of the saints, shook the unsuspecting salesman bodily until his teeth rattled and gave him until sundown to get out of town. The man didn't wait. He went!

Old Clarendon certainly was no Tascosa or Dodge City. Its residents were hand picked, and mostly Northern Methodists at that. There were no shootouts, no murders, no gaudily dressed dancehall girls to liven the quiet nights. Generally, there was peace.

Tascosa, however, was a town of another color.

On September 15, 1881, Arrington, in his report to Adjutant General M.H. King, wrote: "I believe 10 or 15 men stationed at Tascosa in Oldham County could do much service as the County is newly organized and is in the center of a large cow range. Cowboys from New Mexico come into town and shoot, and in fact, take the town. The sheriff sent his family off on account of the lawlessness, and he says from 30 to 40 cowboys often come in and he is powerless to enforce the law. I am satisfied that the leading stockmen in that section sanction such cutting up as it will keep the country from settling up and they can hold their range."

On July 19, 1882, Arrington, stationed to the south in Blanco Canyon, left camp with five men for Tascosa and arrived to find considerable excitement resulting from the murder of Deputy Sheriff Henry McCullar by Mexican Frank Larque, a tough card dealer. Arrington, who called McCullar "McCullough" in his report, said the "murder was entirely unprovoked and cold blooded."

McCullar had come to Tascosa with a tough bunch who had been run out of Mobeetie. He was so mean, in fact, "that he couldn't get along with his own kind."

It wasn't long, however, before McCullar got his comeuppance. A cowboy clouted him so hard with a handgun that McCullar didn't recover for three months, and when he did, he had undergone a complete personality change. He became a respectable citizen and was appointed as a deputy under Sheriff Cape Willingham.

McCullar attempted to arrest Mexican Frank for some gambling irregularity, and the gambler, not taking his gun out, lifted his holster and fired, hitting McCullar in the stomach. The deputy crawled to the home of Jenny, a prostitute he was living with, and, following several days of intense suffering, died. He was buried in Tascosa's Boothill cemetery.

Mexican Frank headed for the New Mexico line with Sheriff Willingham in hot pursuit. The outlaw breakfasted at the Alamocitos Ranch headquarters, and was spotted leaving by Willingham. The law officer circled around in front of the gambler and waited. Watching his back trail, Mexican Frank should have paid more attention to what was in front of him. Willingham stepped out onto the trail.

"That'll be far enough, Frank."

With Willingham's favorite weapon, a shotgun, leveled at his stomach, the outlaw made no unnecessary moves and meekly surrendered.

When the two returned to Tascosa, Mexican Frank was deposited behind bars, and Willingham asked Arrington to assist in guarding him.

"There are a number of gamblers and others of the lowest order making threats of releasing the murderer," Arrington wrote to King.

Promises, promises. Nothing happened, and Mexican Frank was convicted and sentenced to 20 years.

So his company could patrol the Texas Panhandle easier, Arrington established a camp on Sweetwater Creek, two miles east of Mobeetie. "Tascosa," he said, "is the hardest place on the frontier," and he spent a good deal of time seeing that the cowtown stayed as peaceful as possible. In actual fact, Tascosa was no better nor worse than other towns which blossomed along the cattle trails in the 1870s and 1880s. Dodge City, Newton, Wichita, Caldwell, Hays City, Ogallala, Cheyenne, all were wide open towns with reputations for fast gun play, sporting women and quick-dealing gamblers.

Tascosa had its moment in the sun, rising briefly, then setting quickly when the railroad passed it by. At its peak, Tascosa had a population of around 600. Charles F. Rudolph, optimistic editor of the *Tascosa Pioneer,* wrote: "Seven saloons. We Boom." And another time, he wrote: "Business men here remark that the only difficulty about selling goods these days is to get them in as fast as they are demanded."

The town had its shootings, prostitutes, card sharps, religion, formal dances, drama clubs and an atmosphere of serenity that somehow fails to appear in the writings about this Panhandle town.

There were the "respectable portion" and "Hogtown" portion. A sign—"No Shooting Beyond This Line"—separated the two. Vice stayed where the "good" people expected it to stay and law enforcement officers paid as little attention to the goings on as they could.

The infamous Billy the Kid camped under large cottonwoods near Tascosa, but he didn't bother anyone and was left alone.

When the railroad failed to lay its tracks into town, Tascosa faded away. Little remained of the town by 1915.

M.H. King sent Arrington's company to the Panhandle for permanent occupancy in 1882. King was of the opinion that Arrington's camp in Blanco Canyon, "once so important as an outpost against Indians," could now be safely broken up and better service rendered by sending the Rangers north. Waxing somewhat poetic, King observed that the Panhandle "has already reached and conquered the lofty battlements of the once mysterious and dreaded 'Staked Plains,' while the iron lines of trade and travel from the east and west and from the north and south, after spanning the deserts, bridging the rivers and climbing the mountains, have met and joined their mighty forces upon our extreme frontier at the celebrated El Paso del Norte, where the cold red waters of the Rio Grande, in their swift rush from the mountains, divide the two great republics of the North American Continent."

Arrington's Company C was moved to Wheeler County near Mobeetie, a change wished for and earnestly urged by the officials of the upper Panhandle.

By the end of 1882, the Frontier Battalion, which by then had little frontier to protect, was nearing the end of its usefulness. The Rangers had accomplished their purpose. They had tamed the expanding frontier. In *Lone Star, A History of Texas and the Texans,* T.R. Fehrenbach wrote, "They did not entirely end all aspects of the Old West; no heritage of violence so deeply implanted could be so quickly erased. The Rangers changed the social climate from anarchy, where every man looked to himself for pro-

46

tection and his six-gun for judge and jury, to one that was simply violent, but over which the laws of organized society could preside."

Something went out of the Frontier Battalion when Major Jones died. Many of the old Ranger captains resigned, some to ranch, others to take up other business activities and some to become sheriffs or marshals in the counties they protected.

On July 1, 1882, Arrington submitted his resignation to General King and Gov. Roberts:

"I herewith hand you my resignation as Capt. Frontier Battalion. I regret that my affairs are such as to warrant such action, but it is to my interest to do so. I respectfully request that my resignation be accepted to take effect August 31, 1882.

"On offering my resignation I would respectfully call your attention to the fact that Sergt. John Hoffar of this Company (C) has been in the service several years, the greater part of the time as First Sergt., and has made a most efficient officer and being posted as to the condition of affairs of this section, besides having a thorough knowledge of company affairs, I respectfully recommend him to your consideration for promotion."

His resignation was accepted, and Sergeant Hoffar was promoted to First Lieutenant to lead Company C.

Following his resignation from the Frontier Battalion, Arrington applied for a pension for Indian service in the state. He was awarded a pension for service in Company E of the Frontier Battalion from June 1, 1875 to August 31, 1876. The time period does not reflect all the time he spent fighting Indians on the Texas Frontier, though.

General Order Number 8, dated November 18, 1882, reduced the companies of the Frontier Battalion to 15 men each, and the Battalion was dissolved officially on May 26, 1900.

General King, in his report to the Legislature on December 31, 1882, pointed out that the "desire of the best citizens on the border to secure in a civil capacity the services of such officers and men among the Rangers as have been conspicuous for good conduct and ability, has been strikingly manifested lately in the election of Captain G.W. Arrington in Wheeler, Captain C.L. Nevill in Presidio and Captain T.L. Oglesby in Maverick to the office of sheriff in the several counties named; and the selection of Captain G.W. Baylor in El Paso and Sergeant C.B. McKinney in LaSalle as candidates for sheriff in said named counties. The two last named officers were defeated."

Arrington was elected sheriff for four two-year terms.

BIBLIOGRAPHY

Chapter Three

Adjutant General John B. Jones' Report to the Texas Legislature, 1880.

The Buffalo Book, David A. Dary, The Swallow Press Inc., Chicago.

Lone Star, A History of Texas and the Texans, T.R. Fehrenbach, The MacMillan Co., New York.

Maverick Town, The Story of Old Tascosa, John McCarty, University of Oklahoma Press, Norman.

Pink Higgins, The Reluctant Gunfighter and Other Tales of the Panhandle, Jerry Sinise, Nortex Press, Quanah.

The Texas Panhandle Frontier, Frederick W. Rathjen, University of Texas Press, Austin.

The Texas Rangers, Walter Prescott Webb, University of Texas Press, Austin.

Texas Ranger Papers, Reports from G.W. Arrington to Major John B. Jones, University of Texas Archives.

Texas Ranger Sketches, Robert W. Stephens, Dallas, Texas.

AN ARRINGTON FAMILY portrait taken about 1902—Standing, left to right, Sadie (Teas); John and May (Grimes). Seated, left to right, G.W. (Cap) Arrington, French and Mrs. Sarah B. Arrington. Standing, front row, left to right, Orlean (Hoghland), Empress (Bowers) and Inez (Crenshaw).

THE MOBEETIE (Tex.) Jail where Arrington lived while Sheriff of Wheeler County.

CHAPTER FOUR
The John Leverton Case

Charles Goodnight, one of the first cowmen to bring a herd into the Panhandle in 1876, had talked Arrington into running for sheriff. The two had become good friends during Arrington's sojourns into the Panhandle as a Ranger captain.

The frontier was settling down, and with the Kiowas and Comanches on reservations or on the run in other parts of the State, the cowmen, Spanish sheepmen, farmers and merchants started moving into the wide open Panhandle in earnest.

When the Federal census takers came into the Panhandle in 1880 to take the initial counting on the high plains, they registered 1607 Anglos, Spanish and blacks. The big center of population was at Fort Elliott, where 296 soldiers, their families and civilian workers lived. Nearby Mobeetie registered 166 citizens.

The first regular term of the District Court began January 19, 1880, and the first grand jury summed up the conditions in the Panhandle thusly: "This being the first term of the District Court held in the Pan Handle [sic] of Texas, a country heretofore without civil law, the grand jurors have in their investigations confined themselves to the more serious offenses against the laws of Texas.

"The grand jurors are of the opinion that it cannot be expected of a community just settling a new country that the laws concerning public morals have been as strictly complied with as in the more densely populated districts where the laws have been for a long term of years enforced and understood. Nor can it be expected that the mere fact of the civil organization of a county in a remote and unsettled region will immediately reform and correct abuses of the laws of the State concerning misdemeanors. Such reform must necessarily be gradual."

Henry Fleming, saloon owner, educated and honest gambler, was Wheeler County's first sheriff. It was in his saloon that Bat Masterson killed his first white man. Masterson, a faro dealer for Fleming, frequently played poker. A soldier accused Masterson of cheating, pulled a gun and shot Masterson in the stomach. Masterson pulled his pistol and killed the soldier.

Fleming, who once won a herd of 800 cattle in a night of gambling while he was sheriff, was generally ineffective as a law officer. He tried hard, but one man against a town can do little, and the lawless element pretty well had its way until some of the more substantial citizens in town, such as Charles Goodnight, felt it was time to call a halt to it all.

In the summer of 1881, J.N. Browning, with a commission as district attorney from Gov. O.M. Roberts, rode into town. He gathered evidence against the gamblers and arrested as many as he could. His life was threatened, but he ignored the rumblings of discontent. When Browning continued to get anonymous letters, embellished with skulls and crossbones, he took the matter before the county judge, and the judge gathered around him a group of righteous citizens who visited each saloon with an ultimatum. "If anything happens to Browning, every last gambler in town will be hanged from the highest tree." The message was clear, and the gamblers started leaving rather than end up in jail.

When Arrington resigned from the Rangers on August 31, 1882, he hired out as deputy sheriff under Fleming. In November, 1882, Fleming resigned, and Arrington filled his unexpired term, becoming the elected sheriff on January 1, 1883.

Mobeetie's first jail was a two-story structure of cottonwood logs, and one of Arrington's first duties was to build a 10-foot high fence of cedar posts and cottonwood boards around the jail. It was crude, but effective. Prisoners were put into the jail by ladder and the ladder withdrawn once they were inside. Escape was practically impossible.

Arrington also collected $106.30 from the county for serving as jail guard from November 22, 1882 to January 31, 1883. He petitioned the county commissioners to allow him $50 a month to hire a guard, so he could get about his duties elsewhere in the county. The commissioners complied and also allowed him one dollar per day per prisoner for board.

Joe Mason, who was elected sheriff January 1, 1890, was Arrington's deputy.

Arrington did what all sheriffs do. Collect taxes, sell land for taxes, saw to it that the citizens obeyed the laws of the county.

Mobeetie, dubbed the Mother City of the Panhandle, was a wide open town, and despite the efforts of Fleming and Browning, it remained for Arrington to impress the citizens that the law was meant to be obeyed. Since the main entertainment was drinking, gambling and women, nothing new to a developing town in the Old West, Arrington saw to it that the games were honest, the card sharps were moved out of town and the ladies of the evening were hasseled to the point of leaving. Vagrancy then was the same as vagrancy now, and the girls would pay their $15 fines and go back to work until caught again.

Among the crimes investigated by Arrington were theft of horse, unlawfully driving cattle from their accustomed range (a long way of saying, rustling), carrying a pistol, keeping a disorderly house (that one usually ended with a $100 fine), keeping and exhibiting a bank for gaming purposes, assault with intent to rape, assault with intent to murder and murder itself.

The most notable case he investigated resulted in murder charges being brought against him.

"The Grand Jurors . . . upon their oaths present, in the District Court . . . : That one G.W. Arrington . . . did then and there with malice aforethought kill one John Leverton by shooting him . . . with a gun. . . ."

There was no question about it. Arrington shot Leverton with a $300, second hand, double-barrelled, 10-gauge shotgun made by Scott & Sons of Lubbock, Tex. It was his favorite weapon.

Leverton's wife filed murder charges against Arrington, and the case, following a change of venue to Donley County from Oldham County, was tried in Clarendon, Texas.

The events leading to John Leverton's death began more than a year prior when he and his brother, George, moved a small herd of cattle onto LX Ranch range during the summer of 1885. The brothers had gotten permission from John Hollicott, ranch foreman, to run a few head on LX grass, and also permission to live in the old EVN ranchhouse in Evans Canyon, a heavily wooded draw leading toward the Canadian River. Hollicott had told the brothers they were to vacate the property that fall as the LX needed the house for a winter camp.

Fat cattle in those days were trailed to Kiowa, Kansas, 250 miles northeast, for shipment, and when the LX gathered its herd, Hollicott allowed the Levertons to put in what fat steers they had ready. The brothers also furnished one man for the drive.

New Kiowa, incidentally, was a town of three frame houses in March, 1885, but by August the population had grown to 1100 as a result of the coming of the Southern Kansas Railway. There were two newspapers, the Kiowa *Herald,* edited and published by J.M. Simmons, and the *Journal,* published by W.C. Charles. There also was a bank capitalized for $100,000, and a half dozen hotels, serveral frame residences and most important of all, "the largest and best system of stockyards in the state," built by the railway.

The first train of cars into New Kiowa arrived August 9, 1885, and during the succeeding 10 days, cattle shipments amounted to 270 cars averaging 20 cattle per car. The first week's shipments amounted to nearly $11,000.

With the fall drive finished and the cattle shipped, Hollicott and his crew were ready to settle in for the winter. The Levertons, however, refused to allow them to have the house, claiming it was built on a school section and therefore the property of the State. The LX denied it, but rather than have trouble with the brothers, the LX crew camped the winter in a small rock house Evans had built for a blacksmith shop.

"That'll be the last favor from us," Hollicott told the two brothers.

During the spring roundup in 1886, cowboys from the LX and nearby ranches rode into the Canadian River Valley where the Levertons were holding some 250 cattle. The cowboys looked their herd over closely for strays and "burned" cattle. Hollicott cut out three two-year-old steers, claiming they were lost before being branded with 6,000 yearling bought by the company the previous summer. John Leverton protested, but lost the argument.

Suspicion of rustling was nearly as bad as being caught in the act in those early cattle days in the Panhandle, and although there was no proof right then, the feeling was there about the Levertons. Perhaps John and George, not the most hospitable pair, brought this suspicion upon themselves.

The Levertons had worked on most of the big ranches in West Texas. John, not a gunman in the accepted sense, had a reputation of having a quick temper and a fast gun. George was just George, something of a practical joker, but generally regarded as a good cowboy.

The brothers worked for Bill and Bob Yarbo on the J-Y Ranch in Montague County in 1878, then the PUP Ranch on the Pease River in 1879. The PUP, a spread 50 miles northeast of the famous Matador Ranch, was owned by a one-eyed rancher named Steve Rupe. George said Rupe was "as good a man who ever worked." Their pay was $25 a month plus room and board.

On their way to work for Rupe, the Levertons stopped at the mouth of Buffalo Creek in Montague County where Burk Burnett had a camp.

George, talking to a line rider, asked how much Burnett paid him a month.

"About $150. Fifty cash and I waste the rest," the cowboy said.

The PUP sold in 1880 to the Matador, and the two brothers worked for the new owner until the fall of 1881, when they hired out to Charles Goodnight. From there they went to the Diamond F, owned by B.B. Groom. Groom's son, Harrison, operated a ranch south of White Deer, Texas.

Recalling their Diamond F days, George said, "We branded and gathered beef that summer on up to the fall. They branded a mashed 'O'."

Henry Lovitt was the Diamond F's foreman, and George, who always had a story to tell, said, "I'm going to tell you something on Henry. He may not want to own up to it, but he will sure have to come across.

"We camped about two or three miles from the corral above the Diamond F headquarters on the creek, and we had a bunch of gathered beef. We all went down to the house for dinner. There had been three wagons that passed there going north a day or two before that, and they had a Negro cook to do the work around the house, and nobody was there, and this Negro man had a patch of watermelons, about an acre, over on the hill, and taken these people over there and gave them all the watermelons they could carry as they was ripe all over the patch.

"Harrison Groom met them about 200 yards from the patch, just as they left the gate, and said, 'Where did you fellows get them watermelons?' And they said they got them right back there at the house, and he said, 'Then just turn right around and take them back,' and they turned around and taken the watermelons back, and then went on. Directly he come in and told us about it.

"That evening Henry told us not to turn our horses loose, our saddle horses, that he wanted to take a ride. I don't know how many there was of us, but a big bunch of us went down to this watermelon patch and ate watermelons as long as we could, and Henry said, 'Now boys do just like I do,' and he went to pulling up watermelon vines and stomping watermelons, so we done the same. He pulled out his sixshooter, and emptied it, and we all done the same. There wasn't a word said as we rode back to our camp, and we got back Henry said, 'Now, boys, if Harrison comes and says anything about it, send him to me.' "

The Levertons quit the Diamond F and started raising cattle on their own.

Although it had nothing to do with their small cattle operation, George used to tell the following story on himself.

He played a joke on a Mr. Thompson, who lived in Canyon, Texas. "He was a good old religious fellow, and all the preachers went to his house. I lived on the river, had a ranch there, and I had some good grapes that year, so I made a barrel of grape wine, and while making it, I told Old Man Thompson I was going to send him a keg of wine, about 2½ gallons.

"I made the wine, bought a keg, went to a saloon and got a pint of alcohol and poured it in. Then I gave it to Neal McGhee, who carried the mail to Lubbock and had him take it to Mr. Thompson as it was on his way.

"It was Sunday morning that he got there and there was a big meeting going on, and the preachers were all at Thompson's house. Neal drove up to the door and called him out and said, 'Here is a keg of wine George sent you,' and Thompson said, 'Yes, he told me he was going to send some wine,' so he taken it and he and the preachers commenced drinking it, and it wasn't long until meeting time, and when meeting time came, they was all glued to their chairs. I mean they was afraid to get up. I never did tell him about that. Grandma told us that was the funniest joke I ever got off accidentally on them in my life."

The Leverton brand was MEL, purchased from Mel Davis in 1884. Davis started the brand when he was boss of a LIT wagon. During the spring of 1881, Davis was started south with his wagon and crew to work the Texas South Plains for stray LIT cattle. On Running Water Draw, the crew found eighteen head of Mexican cattle, most of them unbranded. Davis branded them MEL, thus going into the cattle business himself. When Bob Robinson, LIT range foreman, saw the newly branded cattle, he fired Davis right then and there.

Davis formed a partnership with three to four other cowboys to brand all unbranded calves and stray cattle they could locate, especially cattle belonging to New Mexico Mexicans that had wandered down the Canadian River. There was a big drift of cattle from the north along the river breaks before fences were built and among them were a number of odd brands no one claimed. Davis and his partners claimed them, and were quite successful at it. Within three years, they had built a large herd. That was about the time the Levertons stepped in and paid $2500 for the brand, and the beginning of their troubles with the LX Ranch and other Panhandle ranches.

Two Turkey Track cowboys reported they met John inside a Turkey Track pasture driving a big calf away from a line camp where the cowboys had been milking the calf's mother. They told John to turn the calf loose and they would forget what they saw. John agreed. Next morning, however, the camp man went out to milk the cow and found the calf inside the pen with "Leverton's brand adorning his side." As one cowboy later observed, "John was hot headed, but he wasn't a fool." One has to believe the cowboys stretched the facts somewhat in retelling the story.

However, a second story coming from the Turkey Track apparently was more fact than fiction and caused Cape Willingham, the ranch's owner, to file charges of cattle theft against the brothers, thus bringing Sheriff Arrington into the story.

A Turkey Track cowboy named Ellington, riding into camp one evening, saw John and George driving a cow and calf toward their Evans Canyon cabin. The cow had hoofs "like a goat's horns," and every cowman in the Panhandle knew her. Not above making a few threats of their own, the Levertons told Ellington that if he mentioned what he had seen "his horse would come in without a rider."

Ellington trailed after them anyway. Because of her hoofs, the cow could not travel too fast and her calf soon gave out. The

Levertons tied the calf and went onto their camp. After dark, Ellington cut an "H" into the calf's hoof so he could identify it later. He then told Willingham what he had seen and done, and the rancher rode into Mobeetie to swear out a warrant for the Levertons' arrest. Cap Arrington formed a posse and headed for the Leverton ranch.

It was 45 miles up the Canadian from the Turkey Track Ranch headquarters to the Levertons' cabin. The posse included Arrington, Willingham, Woods Coffee, Rube Hutton, Mack Sanford and T.N. Adams. They rode until they were four miles from the house, made camp and settled in for the night.

Shortly before dawn, George, unaware that the posse was near, took his dogs and headed toward the nearby caprock to chase down a panther he had heard screaming during the night. Arrington did not know that George had left the cabin.

A thin spiral of smoke came from the rock chimney. Light flickered through the curtained window of one of the cabin's two rooms. Arrington slipped his shotgun from the boot, and the others drew sixshooters or Winchesters, climbed down off their horses and walked quietly toward the cabin door. Arrington checked each man, then cocked the shotgun and kicked the door in.

John was grinding cinnamon bark at the kitchen table. His wife was at the stove cooking breakfast. When the door flew in, they jerked around in startled surprise. John, in desperation, grabbed his pistol from a holster hanging on the end of an unmade bed. He was fast and fired pointblank at Arrington, the first man inside. The bullet scorched Arrington's scarf, setting it afire. Leverton fired again and the bullet ricocheted off the rock wall behind Arrington, hitting Willingham in the calf of his leg and burning a scar across the cheek of Leverton's son lying in a crib against the wall.

Arrington fired, hitting Leverton in the shoulder, three of the large pellets going right through him. Leverton fell. Thinking he had killed him, Arrington moved quickly into the next room, hunting for George. John, bleeding heavily, staggered to his feet and ran outside toward a log crib off to the side of the house. Arrington, returning to the smoke-filled room, ran after him, hollering at him to stop.

"Hold'er there, John!"

Leverton, one arm dangling loose, turned and fired his pistol and kept on running.

"Stop!" Arrington yelled again. Leverton, frantic, kept on going, firing hastily back at the posse. Arrington pulled the trigger and Leverton, mortally wounded, fell 127 paces from the house. He died some four hours later. His wife, Mollie, and George, filed murder charges against the posse, and Arrington and Willingham in particular.

C.F. Rudolph, outspoken editor of the *Tascosa Pioneer,* was outraged at the shooting. In his December 8, 1886, issue, he headlined a story, "Shot Thirteen Times," and wrote that "seeing that his (Leverton's) murder was inevitable, his wife endeavored to get him out and arm him for something of a defense. He then fired five shots himself; whether any of them took affect or not is not known, but it is not believed they did.

"Thirteen shots are said by his brother and brother-in-law of Leverton to have struck him. A messenger was dispatched here for a doctor, but before he reached there, the friends of the murdered man had placed his remains under the sod. . . . Arrington read the warrant for Leverton's arrest after the man to be arrested was in a dying condition, shot thirteen times!"

Rudolph had nothing kind to say about the posse or Arrington. "That an officer of the law could so far forget his duty and his manhood as to arm five deputies and then go beyond the line of his jurisdiction on an errand of deliberate and coldblooded murder seems incredible. But those who have had opportunity to know Arrington best pronounce his reputation in that direction an unsavory one as an officer."

Rudolph, however, left himself an out—just in case he could be wrong. "We do not vouch for the truth of all this in detail, but we give it as we have received it. And we say if the only accounts yet in are anything near correct, whether Leverton were guilty of the smaller offense or not, if there is justice in the Panhandle for redhanded murder, then let justice be done to the utmost."

Writing privately of the shooting, Texas rancher Earl Vandale made it clear it was a dastardly deed.

"John was grinding coffee near the door. Suddenly it was pushed open and Arrington stood there with a shotgun leveled on John. Jumping towards the bedstead on which his sixshooter was hanging, he never had a chance. The second he moved Arrington pulled the trigger and filled him full of buckshot. Arrington never said a word, just pulled the trigger. . . ."

Leverton, according to Vandale's version, got outside, but "only made a few steps when he fell. By that time Old Man English, Leverton's stepfather, got there and assisted Mrs. Leverton to get John into the house and on his bed. As soon as John was shot, Arrington and his posse left for their wagon and the (Turkey Track). On the way down the river, they stopped at L.D. Meek's ranch—who was my father-in-law—and told what had happened. By most people this killing was considered a cowardly uncalled for murder.

"John had heard that they were going to get papers out for his arrest. He sent word to Willingham that anytime he got papers out for his arrest just to send a man after him and he would come in. I think that was the truth, and there was no necessity of taking a strong posse to arrest one man."

Willingham, Vandale wrote, evidently had a guilty conscience. He is said to have hired a gunman by the name of Cooper to act as his body guard. "Everywhere Cape went Cooper was right by his warm side."

Tried, found guilty and ready for the hangman! Feelings ran high. No one was neutral. Arrington, naturally, was not sitting idly by while being tried out of court. He expressed his feelings in a letter to the *Tascosa Pioneer,* complaining "somewhat of the language used by *The Pioneer* in commenting on his killing of John Leverton."

Editor Rudolph, backtracking slightly, said that Arrington "thinks that injustice was done him in the matter in making such comments without having heard his statement in the case. There may be something in this. This paper has no wish to reflect on the conduct of law enforcing officers. . . . The accounts which we had when the article in question was penned then published were the only ones at the time obtainable, and the man who read it saw that the source of that information was the family of the man who was killed. Therefore, we do not see that any injustice was done, only by those parties, whoever they are, that have given out the false account. . . ."

Continuing, Rudolph wrote, "If Leverton stole an animal he should have been arrested; if he resisted arrest he should have been shot. If, on the contrary, he was murdered without a chance to surrender, the duty of every law abiding man would be to see that his murderers, if they were ten times sheriff, were punished to the fullest extent of the law."

Leverton's surviving relatives added to the foment by calling for the Texas Rangers to protect them, claiming in their request to the Adjutant General's office "that it was unsafe for settlers in the Panhandle; that cattlemen and officers were in league to keep them driven out; that they were in danger of being murdered if they attempted to give evidence in these cases."

"Bosh!" exclaimed Rudolph. "No such condition of things exists."

Arrington and Willingham testified before the grand jury in Tascosa on May 1, 1887. Woods Coffee, Rube Hutton, Mack Sanford and T.N. Adams also were there. In their examining trial the four cowboys and Willingham were bound over, with bond set at

$200 each. Arrington's bond was set at $2000. The Oldham County Grand Jury filed a True Bill, No. 306, on May 5, 1887, indicting Arrington for murder. Witnesses before the Grand Jury included W.C. English, Mrs. W.C. English, Mrs. Eva Wells, Cora Leverton and R.A. Spurlock.

A change of venue was granted and trial was held July 8, 1887, in the District Court in Clarendon, Texas. The jurors were D.J. Murphy, Charles Goodnight, J.H. Parks, A.F. Perkins, W.M. Hildebrand, C.H. Taul, J. Shloss, J.H. Combs, Morris Rosenfield, J.E. Pickens, H.W. Taylor and Sam Dyer. Combs was jury foreman.

L.D. Miller was the district attorney prosecuting the case. Defense attorneys were J.H. Woodman and B.M. Barker.

The trial was a short one. The verdict: not guilty.

BIBLIOGRAPHY

Chapter Four

Woods Coffee Jr., Dumas, Texas, interview concerning his father's participation in posse that shot John Leverton.

The Topeka Commonwealth, Topeka, Kansas, August 25, 1885, feature concerning New Kiowa.

District Court Records. Donley County, Texas, Number 157.

District Court Records. Oldham County, Texas, Murder Indictment, Number 306, filed May 5, 1887, State of Texas vs. G.W. Arrington.

The Tascosa Pioneer, December 29, 1886, Panhandle-Plains Museum, Canyon, Texas.

Earl Vandale Papers, ca. 1819-ca.1947, University of Texas Archives, Austin, Texas.

THE OLD ARRINGTON RANCH on the Washita River. In the
photo are the old barn, house and horse pasture to the east.

ROCKING CHAIR RANCHE,
LIMITED

Head Quarter Ranche, Aberdeen, Collingsworth Co. Texas.

189__

LETTERHEAD OF THE Rocking Chair Ranche. G. W. Arrington
was hired to sell the ranch for its English owners.

CHAPTER FIVE

The Rocking Chair Ranche

Cap Arrington knew how to handle hostile Indians, hardened outlaws and cantankerous renegades, but Mrs. J. John Drew was something else. His troubles with her started when he was hired, July 14, 1893, to manage and sell the 252,000-acre Rocking Chair Ranche, headquartered in Collingsworth County.

Arrington's first job was to fire the co-managers, J. John Drew and Archibald John Majoribanks, son of the first Baron of Tweedmouth.

Drew, one associate said, was "a miserable specimen of mankind, with an evil tongue and no sense of humor" and was reputed to "stick to the whiskey bottle." Archibald, Archie or Marshie to those who knew him, was a nonentity. He knew nothing of the cattle business when he arrived from England and apparently didn't want to know anything. The two made a perfect team. Drew set out to enrich his bank account at the Ranche's expense, and Archibald couldn't have cared less, heir apparent to the vast estates of his father notwithstanding.

The Ranche's owners, John Campbell Hamilton Gordon, seventh Earl of Aberdeen, and Edward Majoribanks, eldest son of Sir Dudley Coutts Majoribanks, purchased the ranch in February, 1883 for $161,000. The original deed of trust was executed by Conkle and Lytle on February 17. The purchase included 150,400 acres and 14,745 cattle. By December, 1894, the owners had purchased an additional 1,600 acres and leased 100,000 acres from the State of Texas.

Drew, an opportunist, had been employed by the Cattle Ranch and Land Company at an annual salary of $5,000, and when he heard of the purchase, he sailed to London to organize the Rocking Chair Ranche Company syndicate. He agreed to co-manage the Rocking Chair at a salary of $2,800 with Sir Dudley's youngest son, Archibald, who received a yearly salary of $1,500.

Nobility's Ranch, as its neighbors dubbed it, became a kingdom with Archibald and Drew as its lords and masters. It also became a prime target for rustlers, both outsiders and insiders as it turned out.

Neither Archibald nor Drew was highly regarded. Their tempers were explosive and their drinking excessive. They lived for the moment and gave little consideration to the future.

Settlers moving into the Panhandle had no special feelings for the "foreigners." The big ranches were stumbling blocks to the expanding settlement in the eastern Texas Panhandle, and the settlers had little regard for the rights of the "outsiders." Squatters and nesters took advantage of unscrupulous Drew and the indifferent Archibald. The *Fort Worth Star-Telegram,* on July 15, 1923, expressed the general feeling in an article titled "As Manager of Rocking Chair Ranche Honorable Archie Was A Good Dog Fancier":

"The boys 'up the creek' mavericked the Rocking Chair cattle and made a joke of it, and the hardened co-manager, who was really an Englishman himself but an experienced cattleman and toughened to the trail, mavericked 100 to the settlers' one.

"They stole from the Rockers. Rocking Chair money came in a steady stream, so why not? Archie did not care; apparently nobody cared. There were squatters on alternate sections of school land and there were nesters up on the Elm. They could always sell to the Rockers and get paid in coin of the Realm. They drove bunches down, counted them, delivered them and got their money. Then they drove the cattle over the hill and threw them into a pasture; another outfit took them, drove them around from the other side, sold them and got their money a second time. This process was sometimes repeated until the same bunch of cattle had been sold four or five times."

Drew and Sam Balch, a Rocking Chair cowboy, once were brought into court on charges of "illegally branding one cattle," but a subsequent investigation by the ranch's owners convinced them that the "superintendent and his family had stolen this ranch nearly out of cattle." And that's the situation Arrington started with when he was hired to manage and sell the ranch. The Drews didn't give up without a struggle.

Arrington received power of attorney to handle ranch affairs on August 8, 1893, and on the 12th assumed control from Drew. The former co-manager told Arrington that on July 1, he had leased about 13 sections to some of his former employees, who had filed on and settled school sections in the southeast corner of the ranch. Arrington didn't object to that, but did protest and refuse to recognize a lease of nine sections to Drew's son, J.J. Jr. The lease included the headquarters, corrals, horsepastures and hayfields. Drew stood by the lease, but Arrington examined county records and found nothing to indicate a legal transaction between father and son. He informed Drew to get his family off the ranch.

Meanwhile, Arrington started shipping cattle, and during his absence, Drew Jr. took possession of the horse pasture by turning in some cattle. Arrington moved the cattle out and told the Drews to leave the ranch right then. They did. Then Drew Jr. sent in a bill for $233.36, money he said he paid for the lease on the nine sections. He wanted it back. Arrington refused to pay it.

On July 24 the Farmers Loan & Trust Co., New York, had been notified not to honor drafts drawn by Drew and Archibald after that date. Apparently Drew and Archibald failed to get word of the notice and kept writing checks up through August 5 for labor, provisions and the like. The checks bounced. Arrington wrote new ones and paid off most of the ranch's creditors. Among the checks was one drawn July 25 in favor of the State of Texas for interest on Section 18 due August 1 of each year. The check failed to show up in bank statements and Arrington, fearing that the section, which contained the headquarters buildings, would be forfeited for nonpayment of interest, went to Austin to find that J.J. Drew Jr. had filed his application to purchase the Section 18 "as an actual settler. I prevented that by paying the interest at once," Arrington wrote to the owners. He also sought legal advice on the father and son leasing claims and found them illegal.

Then Mrs. Drew refused to move from the headquarters house.

Arrington had written to Drew that he had leased the headquarters house to L. Smith Gragg, his new range boss, and wanted the Drews out of the place so Gragg could move in. He wrote the letter on December 8, stating the one year lease was to begin January 1, 1894.

Mrs. Drew claimed to have a lease on the house until April 1. The owners informed Arrington that her claim was false and that the Drew lease ended December 31.

Mrs. Drew refused to move, so Arrington filed suit to have her ejected. "She has again stirred up the settlers, and I fear that if she does not leave Aberdeen (the headquarters) the house will be destroyed by fire. Lately poison has been thrown over the fence into the road and a number of settlers dogs have been poisoned. Besides her tongue is a perfect terror. Will advise you as to the result of the trial of detainer," he wrote to the owners.

The problem still hadn't been solved by April. Arrington offered to pay her $75 "for improvements to Aberdeen and to pay Drew Jr. the amount lease paid by him to the company provided he would give a receipt in full of all claims against the company." They refused his offer.

Then, Arrington brought a suit of "forcible detainer" against her and obtained a judgment. She appealed and "on account of not having the 'Articles of Incorporation' of the company on file with the Secretary of State, the judge threw us out of court." Arrington filed a writ of sequestration, but before the writ was served, Mrs. Drew capitulated and offered to leave if Arrington would pay her son. He did, and they did, leaving the property in poor condition. "The cistern and well were in very filthy condition as Mrs. Drew had fed cattle and horses in the yard . . . for several months. On the 29th April a cyclone passed Aberdeen and entirely demolished the Co. blacksmith shop and blew down the yard fence besides breaking out a number of window glass." Arrington cleaned and repaired the headquarters and Gragg moved in.

Once the Drew situation was settled, Arrington should have been able to relax and get down to the major task of selling the Rocking Chair cattle and land, but impatient sodbusters caused him considerable trouble. Farmers had started moving in in earnest, and with an intensifying feeling that the big ranches were too big and fair game for settling. The Rocking Chair was a case in point. Animosity reached the gunshooting and harassment state. Someone burned a large stack of Johnsongrass hay on the ranch and the fire spread into some nearby horse corrals, killing nearly 65 horses. Pastures were set afire and snipers stationed themselves outside the ranch headquarters to take shots at anyone trying to get to the fires to put them out.

Whether Drew was behind the trouble is a matter of speculation. The London, England management hired investigators to learn who was causing trouble, but were unable to pin the blame on any one person.

Arrington ignored the trouble as best he could. Writing to Edward Marjoribanks, he said the cost to run the ranch for twelve months would total $16,250—$8,500 labor, $3,750 taxes and $4,000 lease. Revenue would total $29,500—$8,000 sales of cattle, $15,000 pasturing of 10,000 cattle at $1.50 per head, and $6,500 lease. Pastures were not in good shape because of the "loose management," but with proper rotation they could be improved.

"During the last eight months a financial emergency has existed over the U.S. equal to a panic, consequently real estate has very little value and I am of the opinion that it will be several years before there is any sale for lands in this section of the state, and am firmly convinced that you could not sell this pasture at $1.00 per acre at present, nor the best section for $1.50 cash. I know of thousands of acres that can be bought for $1.00 per acre. By taking cattle to pasture a few thousand dollars can be made above running expenses, lease and taxes, do not believe as much could be made by leasing out the pasture," Arrington wrote.

He suggested they stock young steers. "The pasture will carry 10,000 two year old steers in addition to pasturing enough cattle to pay running expenses. Steers of this class can be purchased at from $12.00 to $13.00 per head and at three years old will sell from $16.00 to $20.00. Nearly all the large ranches have stopped breeding cattle and are stocking with steers. I am fully aware of the fact that the company has lost heavily in the past, all of which could have been avoided by proper management and fair dealing."

Under Arrington's management, the Rocking Chair showed considerable improvement. Cattle were being shipped, accounts due the Ranche were settled and prospective buyers of land were interviewed, among them Dan Waggoner Sr. of Fort Worth.

His interest stirred up a storm among the small cattlemen. They didn't want him running a ranch in Collingsworth County. He ignored them.

Seeing that words weren't enough, the small ranchers burned the headquarters ranchhouse to the ground. Albert Laycock, a bachelor cowboy, lived in another Rocking Chair house on Elm Creek, and before the irate ranchers burned it, they pulled his belongings out into the yard. Laycock had been showing Waggoner around, and when they returned to Laycock's house, the only thing standing was the chimney.

Waggoner headed back to Aberdeen to talk with Arrington, and while he was there, someone burned a barn and came near to burning down the ranchhouse. Waggoner got the message. He went home, forgetting about buying the Collingsworth ranch.

The Continental Land and Cattle Co., the same firm that operated the Mill Iron, bought the Rocking Chair Ranche. The sale was approved at a general meeting of the board in London on October 11, 1896. On December 22, the special warranty deed was signed by Tweedmouth and Aberdeen granting the Continental Land and Cattle Co. ownership of 238 survey of land of 640 acres each for $75,200, a considerable loss to its owners. Archibald's admonition in 1890 to hold onto the land and "not to be in too great haste to get rid of the goose that will lay the golden eggs for us" turned into a costly omelet for the syndicate.

Sir Dudley Coutts Marjoribanks died two years before the sale was completed. Edward Marjoribanks suffered heavy losses in the transaction. Archibald John returned to England with his young American bride in 1897, and died in 1900, "after having been an invalid for many years."

The story of Nobility's Ranche, a kingdom mismanaged by J. John Drew and Archibald John, ended with its sale. Arrington returned to managing his own ranch near Canadian, Texas.

BIBLIOGRAPHY

Chapter Five

Letters written by G.W. Arrington to Edward Majoribanks and John Campbell Hamilton Gordon, owners of the Rocking Chair Ranche Company, Ltd., London, England.

Nobility's Ranche, A History of the Rocking Chair Ranche, Estelle D. Tinkler, BA, West Texas State Teachers College, Canyon, Texas, Master's Thesis, August, 1941.

A GATHERING OF FRIENDS—Standing, back row, left to right: John A. Chambers, Sam Isaacs, J. C. Studer, the next two are unknown, and G. W. (Cap) Arrington; NEXT ROW, l-r: Frank R. Jamison, J. L. Jennings, Dick Bussell, J. S. Hood, Dick Rathjen, unknown, W. C. Isaacs, Judge B. M. Baker (First State Supt. of Public Instruction), Vas Stickley, W. J. Todd. SEATED, l-r: Miss Capitola Garlach, Mrs. George Gerlach, George Gerlach, Mrs. Gerlach, mother of George, Mrs. John Gerlach and the last, unknown.

CHAPTER SIX

The Shooting of Tom McGee

Hemphill County Sheriff Tom McGee died between 11 p.m. and midnight, November 24, 1894, in his Canadian, Texas, home.

According to the autopsy, performed by Dr. A.M. Newman, he had been shot from behind, the fatal bullet entering his right hip, ranging upward, forward and to the left, with the ball lodging two inches below and to the left of his navel.

Two bullet holes were found burned through the right side of the sheriff's short coat, both entering from the front.

Few, if any, townspeople disliked Sheriff McGee. A native of West Virginia, the sheriff had lived in Colorado for several years before moving to the Texas Panhandle to ranch with Henry Cresswell on the Canadian River. About 1886, he bought an interest in the Moody-Andrews Cattle Company, and when the county was organized in 1887, he was elected sheriff by a comfortable majority.

He ran again in 1889 and was elected by a larger majority.

The Canadian Free Press, in its June 14, 1889, issue, said: "He is perhaps as well known and as popular as any man we have in the Panhandle, and known all over the country as one of the straightest and most honorable men in it."

The occasion for this flowery comment was the wedding announcement of the sheriff to Miss Mary Blandy Taylor, niece of Mr. and Mrs. George T. Lynn of Kansas City, Missouri. The two were married June 5, 1889, in the Lynn home.

Said *The Canadian Free Press:* "His many friends will be glad to learn that he has settled down in life with such a worthy mate and will congratulate him and wish them both a long and happy wedded life." Their marriage was relatively short-lived, however. A few months past their fifth anniversary, the well-liked sheriff was dead.

Canadian became a town on Sunday, July 7, 1889, and within sixty days was the major town of any importance in the two year old county. It was a ranching community to begin with, and, with the exception of oil discoveries in the area, remains ranch-oriented even today. It was laid out at the confluence of the Canadian River and Red Deer Creek.

The Santa Fe Railway built a wood frame depot, 80 feet long, 24 feet wide, with a 300-foot long platform, extending an entire block to Purcell Avenue, on the west side of town.

Harm and Ludwick, the *Canadian Free Press* editors and publishers, called the growing community "the Hercules of the Southwest," a somewhat optimistic and exaggerated cognomen as the town never assumed the proportions of that superhuman Greek hero.

The town boasted of three hotels, the Denver, DePeet and Sutherland. Col. George B. Berry, saloon owner, also built an opera house. Other saloons were owned by J.W. Phillips, Paul Hoefel, John Preston, Ernest Welters.

Almond & Alexander of Kingman, Kansas, operated a flour and feed business. J.E. Montgomery of Mobeetie owned a newsstand and stationery store. Hardwick & Cattell owned a bottling works. J.C. Carson advertised his restaurant as "a house built by the Arm of the Lord where the hungry and thirsty may get their fill." S.P. Fulton of Kiowa, Kansas, opened a drayage firm.

There were Walsh's City Bakery & Restaurant, Shaller's Bazaar, Snider's Real Estate, Delaney's Candy Manufacturers and Joseph Heina's bank. Canadian was an active community.

It is unlikely that the death of Sheriff McGee was planned. He happened unknowingly into a robbery that had been planned nine days prior when George Isaacs, Tulsa Jack (alias Will Blake, Joe Blake, Sam Blake), Jim Harbolt and Dan McKenzie met in the Chickasaw Nation to plot the break-in of a Wells Fargo safe and the assault of A.B. Harding, agent, in Canadian. When Sheriff McGee arrived at the train station just as the robbery was about to begin, the thieves altered their plan somewhat. Perhaps they panicked, and if they did, their fright was fatal to McGee.

Isaacs masterminded the safe robbery, starting the project when he walked into Wells Fargo's office in Kansas City's Union Depot and asked the rate for sending money to Canadian, Tex.

A.A. Reinhart, Wells Fargo's money clerk, told him it was "$1.50 per $1,000."

Acknowledging the price, Isaacs walked out. That was November 15, 1894. Two days later, or at least between November 15 and November 20, Isaacs returned and asked Reinhart for several money envelopes. The clerk gave him half a dozen, and he again left the office.

A few hours later, sometime between 6 p.m. and 7 p.m., the Texas cowman returned with five of the envelopes sealed with mucilage. He had written "$5,000" on the corner of each.

"Stitch'em and put the Wells Fargo Public Seal on them," Isaacs told Reinhart. The money clerk did.

"You know, I can give you a better rate because of the large amount," Reinhart said. "Instead of $1.50, the price will be $1.25 per $1,000."

"Okay," Isaacs answered, and handed the clerk $31.25 to ship the envelopes to Canadian.

Reinhart did not count the money. It was Wells Fargo's policy to take a man at his word, and if Isaacs said there was $5,000 in each envelope, that's the way it was. Following procedure, Reinhart called Charles W. Stockton, the company's division superintendent in Kansas City, and told him about the large shipment of money. The time was 7:30 p.m.

"Is he sending the money to a bank?" Stockton wanted to know.

"No. To himself," Reinhart answered.

Stockton hesitated, then shrugged. There was nothing there that seemed out of the ordinary. Money in large sums usually was sent to the cattlemen's banks, but it wasn't uncommon to send it to one's self. He approved the shipment, and wired a Mr. Barnes, superintendent of the Southern Kansas Railroad, to have a car sent through to Canadian. He then telegraphed his route agent, Andrew T. Payne, in Wichita, telling him a car would be coming through with $25,000 aboard and to put a guard on the safe at Wellington, Kansas. The combination of the safe was wired to Harding in Canadian.

Wellington was 265 miles south of Kansas City, and no problems were expected between those two cities.

Jim T. Stockton, a running helper (an assistant to a Wells Fargo messenger) was tapped for guard duties on the $25,000. Normally, Stockton worked the day run between Newton, Kansas and Cleburne, Texas, and from Newton to Guthrie, Texas on the night run. This was his first assignment as a guard. Wells Fargo provided him with a 32 calibre pistol on a 45 calibre frame and a 10 gauge double barrelled Remington shotgun. He boarded the train at Winfield Junction, Kansas, a stop 28 miles north of Wellington, and stayed in the baggage car with the safe.

The trip to Canadian was uneventful. Engine 203 pulled its one passenger car and baggage car into the Texas Panhandle town. The express car was switched to the north side of the drab-colored depot. A few spectators stood around, some to watch the train puff its way up and down the track, others to see friends off. The engine, wheezing and clanking, took on water and coal.

"Boaaard!"

The passengers climbed aboard, among them "Cap" Arrington and his friend, Cape Willingham, both heading for Panhandle, Texas.

Under the watchful eyes of Stockton and Agent Harding, Isaac's five money envelopes were taken from the baggage car safe and transferred to the Wells Fargo safe inside the Canadian station. Harding, still jittery from a robbery at the station a couple nights before, sent someone for Sheriff McGee.

"Stay around until he gets here will ya," he asked Stockton.

"Sure," the guard answered. He loosened the pistol in its holster and checked the loads in his shotgun. Harding felt a little better at this show of gunpower and Stockton's apparent confidence.

Wearing a short coat against the evening chill, Sheriff McGee came striding into the station.

"Howdy," he nodded to Harding. He paused briefly to talk with Stockton.

"We'd feel a lot safer if you'd deputize a couple of men to stay through the night, Sheriff," Stockton said.

"Okay. Let me see if there are any loafers around outside first." He stepped out onto the wooden platform. Harding and Stockton, satisfied with the protection the money was to have that night, visibly relaxed as they watched the sheriff shove through the doorway. He had no sooner passed from sight when he was shot!

Six to 10 shots were fired, apparently none of them by the surprised sheriff.

"Wha' the . . . !" Stockton, cocking the shotgun, ran outside, keeping low. He saw nothing, then saw the sheriff down, holding his leg.

"My leg . . . my leg!" the sheriff gasped.

Grabbing him as best he could and still holding his shotgun ready, Stockton helped the wounded officer to a cot in the freight room.

"You see anybody?" Stockton asked.

"Not for sure . . . seemed I'd seen him before . . . maybe in town during the day . . . small man . . . small."

Harding, meanwhile, had gotten Doc Newman. He tried to save the sheriff. He couldn't and the man died three hours later.

The killing shocked the town council into special session.

"Get Arrington!" someone suggested, and a telegram was sent right then. Arrington had arrived in Panhandle by then, but caught the first train back, a stock train that came through the small farm community about 3 a.m. The town council met him when the train pulled in, told him what happened.

Arrington told the upset men he'd remain on the station platform until daylight to prevent anyone from going on the north side of the track and obliterating the trail of the outlaws.

"Get Sam Isaacs for me will you," he asked.

Sam showed up a little while later. "Where's George?" Arrington wanted to know.

"Haven't seen him."

"You know of anyone who might have known about the big

70

money shipment?"

"No one but the family," Sam said.

George couldn't be found.

Daylight came slowly. When it finally came, Arrington took up the trail. A lawman for better than 15 years and an experienced tracker, he knew what to look for. He saw where a man had jumped off a platform at the end of a railroad car at the back of the depot. Boot heel marks showed the man to be "small." Arrington came across the tracks of a second man and followed them to the front of the Fay House. The tracks separated, finally coming together with a third set of footprints. Arrington followed them to the stockyards, where their horses had been tied. Apparently a fourth man had stayed with the horses, tied from six to eight feet apart along the heavy fence.

The four outlaws hit the edge of town at a gallop. Arrington headed a posse that took off after them. They trailed them to where they had cut Studer's fence, then down to old Dan McKenzies in D County, Oklahoma [now Ellis and Roger Mills Counties]. Then the outlaws crossed the river and the posse lost the trail.

"You-all go on back. I'll see if I can pick it up again."

The posse turned back, and Arrington urged his horse into the shallow river. He returned four days later to find George Isaacs in the Canadian jail.

The Hemphill County Grand Jury, impaneled during the May, 1895, term, agreed that Isaacs "did . . . with malice aforethought kill Tom T. McGee by shooting him . . . with a pistol" on November 23, 1894. Included in the indictment were Tulsa Jack, Jim Harbolt and Dan McKenzie.

Isaacs wasn't about to stay in jail if he didn't have to. He wanted out and filed a writ of habeas corpus saying he was being "illegally detained" by the deputized Arrington. His petition, dated May 22, 1895, was to the Honorable B.M. Baker, judge of the 31st Judicial District of Texas.

> Sir = I am illegally confined and restrained of my liberty at Canadian in Hemphill County in the jail thereof by G.W. Arrington, sheriff . . . I pray your honor to grant and issue a writ of habeas corpus to have me forthwirth brought before your honor to the end that I may be discharged from such illegal confinement. . George Isaacs

Witnessing Isaacs' signature was J.H. Hopkins, District Clerk, Hemphill County.

The hearing on Isaacs' petition was held in chambers before the Honorable J.M. Hurt, judge of the Court of Criminal Appeals, in

Canadian on September 6, 1895. The hearing caused quite a sensation!

Twelve witnesses were called—C.W. Jones, a Brown County rancher; Fred Hosburgh, Canadian; J.J. Sutherland, owner of the Sutherland House; Willie Sutherland, his son; G.W. Fishburn, assistant cashier, First National Bank, Kansas City, Mo.; A.A. Reinhart, foreman, Wells Fargo Express Co., Kansas City Union Depot.

And Charles W. Stockton, Wells Fargo Division Superintendent, Kansas City; Andrew T. Payne, route agent, Wells Fargo, Wichita, Kansas; J.T. Stockton, Wells Fargo guard; N.J. Overstreet, Wells Fargo agent, Canadian; Dr. A.M. Newman, physician and surgeon, Canadian; G.W. Arrington, rancher, and D.J. Young, cashier, Canadian Valley Bank.

TESTIMONY OF C.W. JONES

On the night of November 23, Jones was on the train heading back toward Amarillo. He had delivered a herd of cattle in Gage, Oklahoma Territory, that day.

"When the train arrived in Canadian, I got off to eat supper at Paul Hoefel's Cafe, located next to the station. I don't know how long the train stopped here, but I think from 20 minutes to half an hour."

ATTORNEY: Now do you know the defendant here, George Isaacs?

"I used to know him. I haven't seen him for about 10 years. He was on the train that evening."

ATTORNEY: What attracted your attention to this defendant if you saw him. What was he doing?

"Well, when I got on the train at Gage, Mr. Barber was on there coming from Kansas City. When I came in, I sat down by Mr. Barber. I noticed the gentleman on the opposite side of the aisle sitting just behind where Mr. Barber was sitting, but I didn't recognize him."

ATTORNEY: Do you recognize this defendant as the man you saw there?

"I don't know that I do. When we got here to Canadian, as we got up to go out of the car, this man sitting opposite of us passed down the aisle ahead of us. I remarked to Mr. Barber, 'Is that Bill Isaacs?' as he walked out ahead of us. Another gentleman said it was Sam. I knew it wasn't Sam as Sam was a taller man than that."

ATTORNEY: Did you notice what direction he went off in? What side of the train did he get off?

"I don't know. I never paid any attention to him."

ATTORNEY: You say you had known the defendant eight or ten

years before.

"Yes, sir. I have not seen him since '83 or possibly '84. I recog nized him as Bill.

ATTORNEY: Is there much resemblance between the Isaacs brothers?

"Yes, sir."

TESTIMONY OF FRED HOSBURGH

Hosburgh was at the Sutherland Hotel reading when the train pulled in. He saw George Isaacs come into the hotel and register. Isaacs asked Sutherland if Sam was staying there, then went on up the stairs where Sutherland showed him to his room.

ATTORNEY: When he came in you knew he was an Isaacs by his resemblance?

"When I heard him call for Sam Isaacs, I saw the resemblance."

ATTORNEY: You know Bill Isaacs, Sam Isaacs and the other brother?

"Yes, sir."

ATTORNEY: Well, why didn't you take him to be one of them?

"I had never seen this man before, but I knew he was not either of them."

Hosburgh didn't see George after Sutherland took him to his room until the next day. Sam introduced George to Hosburgh about dinner time in the Sutherland Hotel.

ATTORNEY: Could a person that night have gone from a bedroom upstairs and out of the hotel without going through the office or without you knowing it from where you was sitting in the office?

"Well, if he had his boots off and had been right quiet about it, he might have done it."

TESTIMONY OF J.J. SUTHERLAND

Sutherland had been attending a Christian Endeavor meeting when the Southern Kansas rolled into Canadian. It was his habit to meet the train with his wagon to pick up possible hotel guests, but on this night, he sent his son, Willie, instead. When he arrived at the hotel following the CE meeting, Hosburgh, a Mr. Stokes and a stranger were waiting in his office. Willie told his father the gentleman wanted a room, and Sutherland put the man in Room 28 in the center part of the hotel's main hall. Stokes was given Room 17.

"I came down and went over to Johnson's, and just as I was going to put my foot on the platform I heard the shooting."

ATTORNEY: About how far is Johnson's from your house?

"One hundred feet."

ATTORNEY: About what length of time elapsed from the time

you left the room until you got across the street?

"Four or five minutes."

The Sutherland Hotel was about three blocks from the train depot, something over 1,000 feet, and Hoefel's Cafe was about 150 feet from the depot.

ATTORNEY: From the time you took this defendant to his bedroom and the time you left the building could he have got out of the house without you knowing it?

"No, sir."

The State cross-examined Sutherland.

PROSECUTOR: How many minutes did it take from the time you left Mr. Isaacs' room until you came down and got Mr. Stokes and showed him up to his room and got back to the foot of the stairs?

"About 10 minutes."

PROSECUTOR: Did you go right to Johnson's?

"From the time I left Stokes, it can't have been more than five minutes until I got over to Johnson's."

Willie Sutherland had taken the wagon to the station that night, but Isaacs apparently chose to walk to the hotel. The first time Willie saw him was in the hotel office.

"The only passenger I had was Mrs. Bill Isaacs and I drove her home. I had asked Mr. Isaacs if he had come in on the train, and he said he had. Then I asked him why he didn't come up with me in the wagon. He said he had gotten off to mail a letter and walked to the hotel."

TESTIMONY OF G.W. FISHBURN

As assistant cashier of the First National Bank in Kansas City, Fishburn remembered seeing George Isaacs in the bank during November, "about the 22nd." Isaacs had come into the bank to cash a check.

"He had one of the Drumm Flato Commission Company's checks and he took it to the teller, who asked him for identification. He was referred to me, and I suggested that Mr. Isaacs go back to the office of Drumm Flato Commission Company and endorse the check, then have the endorsement okayed by one of the company officials. He did, and he brought it back and we cashed it."

ATTORNEY: Did Mr. Isaacs make any statement at the time as to what kind of money he wanted?

"He expressed a wish for small money. The teller offered him some currency, and he said that something smaller would be more convenient for him as he was going to trade with Indians. I got a package of $500 of one and two dollar bills and handed it to the teller, and he immediately handed it over to Mr. Isaacs. Isaacs said anything would do for the balance of the check."

ATTORNEY: Do you remember the amount of the check?
"$689 and something."

Damaging evidence started piling up against Isaacs. A.A. Reinhart, Wells Fargo's money clerk, saw Isaacs "between the 15th and 20th of November" and received from Isaacs "five packages addressed to 'Geo. Isaacs, Canadian, Tex.' Each package was marked in the corner, '$5,000.00.' "

Reinhart never counted the money, "because we have instructions not to count any money shipped."

Division Superintendent Charles W. Stockton, later a Wells Fargo vice president, corroborated Reinhart's statement. "It was unusual for money shipments of that size to be sent to individuals rather than banks and specially to a place the size of Canadian. In fact, it was unusual even to send it to the bank in a town the size of Canadian."

One of the State's witnesses was unable to testify "because he is at Cripple Creek (Colorado) investigating a stage robbery." His name was Fred Dodge, an undercover investigator with Wells Fargo. Dodge, a dead ringer for Morgan Earp of the famous Earp brothers, was sent to Canadian by a Mr. Andrews, manager of Wells Fargo's Central Department in Kansas City. He talked with Isaacs about the attempted holdup and shooting. With him was Cap Arrington.

Arrington said Isaacs told Dodge that "he didn't expect the train to be jumped at Canadian, but expected it would be between Higgins and Canadian. There was no specific place mentioned." Isaacs also told Dodge that he hired three men to hold up the depot.

TESTIMONY OF JIM T. STOCKTON

When the train arrived in Canadian, the money was taken out of the express car safe and put into the safe in the depot. The express car was switched to the north size of the station.

"I asked Tom McGee to deputize a couple of men to stay with me at the depot that night, but he told me his two deputies were out of town. I asked the sheriff if he thought there would be any danger and he said he didn't think so. Just after he went out of the depot, I heard some shooting."

The shots fired at the sheriff came close together, all seemingly fired within 30 seconds or so. Stockton ran to the door and found the sheriff "staggering over the sill of the waiting room door." He got the sheriff onto a cot in the freight room. The sheriff told him that when he stepped outside, he "met the man and the man began firing immediately."

ATTORNEY: Did you see any parties during the time of the

shooting?

"No, sir."

ATTORNEY: You say you stayed all night at the depot? And all the next day? Did you see the defendant the next day?

"I saw him in the office there, and the agent, Mr. Harding, introduced him to me as Mr. Isaacs, the man that owned the shipment of money."

ATTORNEY: Do you know whether or not the packages you had guarded were delivered to him or not?

"Yes, sir."

TESTIMONY OF N.J. OVERSTREET

Overstreet, Wells Fargo operator and clerk, said the train arrived in Canadian "about 7:50 p.m., and remained there from a half to three-quarters of an hour."

ATTORNEY: Did you see any parties around the depot?

"Yes, sir. I saw some strangers around the depot part of the time. I didn't recognize any of them."

When Isaacs came to the station the next morning to pick up the five envelopes, Overstreet said he heard Isaacs and Harding discussing the money. "I don't know what he said he was going to do with the envelopes. He wanted to leave them there for some reason."

ATTORNEY: Did he say anything about reshipping any of it?

"He spoke of wanting to reship some of it after he had received it. He said he would bring it back that evening to reship the next morning. Mr. Harding said he would not receive that amount to hold over night as it was the instructions of the Company not to hold any large amount of money over night. I saw Isaacs take the envelopes and sign a receipt for them."

Sam Isaacs was with him at the time.

TESTIMONY OF D.J. YOUNG

Young was a cashier in the Canadian Valley Bank. He hadn't heard the shots fired, but was in front of Gerlach's Building when some boys came running up the street and said some men were holding up the depot. "They said that McGee was shot." Young was among those who went into Gerlach's and got some guns and ran toward the depot.

ATTORNEY: Have you seen these packages before?

"The first time I saw them was in the room back of the old Traders Bank on Sunday evening. I believe it was the 25th of November."

ATTORNEY: What did you do with the packages?

"Sam Isaacs gave them to me wrapped up in a newspaper. I opened them and counted the contents."

ATTORNEY: Was the defendant, George Isaacs, present when

76

you opened the packages?

"He was. We opened the packages and I counted part of the contents and Mrs. Thompson the rest. I found one hundred dollars of one and two dollar bills in each package. A total of $500.00."

ATTORNEY: What was done with the money?

"It was turned over to Sam Isaacs, and the packages were put in the safe deposit box."

TESTIMONY OF G.W. (CAP) ARRINGTON

Arrington, a rancher and also manager of the Rocking Chair Ranche, had been in Canadian on business on November 23. He was on his way to the depot to catch the train for Panhandle when he met a man "about 20 steps this side of Paul's." He didn't recognize him at the time.

The man passed the former Texas Ranger, then turned and asked, "Where's there a hotel?" Arrington pointed to the Fay House across from where the two were standing.

ATTORNEY: Was he coming in the direction of the Sutherland Hotel?

"He was coming up the street. He was walking rapidly enough that he attracted my attention."

Arrington caught the train, went on to Panhandle, then caught the 3 a.m. stock train back to Canadian when the telegram from the town council reached him.

When he arrived, he asked that Sam Isaacs come to the depot.

"Where's George, Sam?"

"In town."

"Find him and ask if anyone knew he was going to ship this money."

Sam knew of no one who did, but he went off to find George.

Meanwhile, Jim Stockton had joined Arrington on the station platform, and after exchanging greetings, Arrington wanted to know where the money had come from and how much there was.

"I want to know all about it," he told Stockton.

When the guard said it came from George Isaacs and that there was $25,000, Arrington observed that "he knew George."

When daylight came Arrington and the posse took up the trail.

ATTORNEY: State the condition you found the tracks in in the morning as soon as it got light enough to see.

"I saw where one man had jumped off the platform at the end of a car at the back of the depot. I trailed them back of the Fay House and the trail crossed the road that runs north, then there were three of them. The third man had run in front of the Fay House. The tracks went to the stockyards where they had their horses tied. One man had stayed with the horses."

Arrington and the posse followed the galloping horses to the river and lost the trail there. The posse returned and Arrington went on, spending four or five days in Oklahoma Territory trying to track the killers down. When he returned, he found George Isaacs in jail, and willing to talk.

ATTORNEY: Did Isaacs promise that he would help catch the others if you would release him?

"Yes, sir. Dodge had a talk with him, and the promise was made in jail. Dodge, Stickey and Hoover and I and Bill Isaacs were there when the promise was made. He told us he could get them in two weeks.

ATTORNEY: You gave him two weeks?

"Yes, sir."

ATTORNEY: After he had gone you swore out another complaint and charged him with murder?

"Yes, sir."

ATTORNEY: He was not charged with murder this first time?

"No. He was charged with conspiracy to commit robbery. He waived an examining trial and put up $5,000 bond."

Isaacs left town after telling Arrington the other members of the gang were "Stanley, Bill Doolin and Bitter Creek."

ATTORNEY: Has the grand jury of this county indicted these parties?

"No, sir."

ATTORNEY: Have you any reason to believe they were here?

"No, sir."

ATTORNEY: Do you know they were not here?

"I am well satisfied of it."

Although the Doolin Gang was suspect, Arrington didn't believe for a moment they were involved in the robbery attempt. Isaacs lied, and Arrington knew it. Arrington knew the Doolin bunch—Bill Doolin, "Little Bill" Raidler, George (Red Buck) Waightman, George (Bitter Creek) Newcomb, Charles Pierce, Dick (Little Dick) West, Tulsa Jack, Dynamite Dick and Arkansas Tom. The robbery didn't have the feel of the Doolin Gang.

Tulsa Jack possibly free-lanced the Canadian robbery attempt, and was the only member of the gang involved. Six months following the Canadian shooting, Tulsa Jack was killed during a train robbery at Dover.

Author Glenn Shirley in *Six-Gun and Silver Star* quotes a dispatch from El Reno, Oklahoma to the Guthrie (Oklahoma) *Daily Leader,* dated November 28, 1894, concerning the shooting:

A package purporting to contain $25,000 was expressed from Kansas City to George Isaacs, a wealthy Chickasaw cattleman at Canadian, Texas, arriving at that point Saturday evening last.

When the train pulled into Canadian station, a gang of bandits held up the train. Sheriff McGee, of that county, was standing by and took a hand at the shooting in the protection of the express company, and was killed by the robbers, being literally shot to pieces, and several others were fatally wounded in the engagement, among them being some of the robbers, who were carried away by their pals.

The robbers were frightened off without securing anything, and were chased into the Wichita Mountains and the Butte lands of the Wichita country . . . and a large force of officers are out from these points looking for the bandits.

Isaacs, who shipped the money, was arrested on suspicion of complicity and taken to Texas. The scheme is supposed to be shipment of money that was to be stolen, and the express company made to disgorge and proceeds to be divided. A number of wealthy cattlemen of the Chickasaw Indian nation probably furnished the capital of $25,000 to begin business on. . . .

So much for truth in reporting. Interesting, but hardly accurate, or as is said in the newspaper trade, "the writer didn't allow facts to get in the way of a good story."

In a footnote in the same book, Shirley writes: "In *Outlaw Days,* pp. 76-78, and again in *Marshal Of The Last Frontier,* p. 210, Zoe A. Tilghman credits the Doolin gang with this robbery and killing of Sheriff McGee. Nix makes no such connection in *Oklahombres,* and Bill Tilghman himself, in listing to Fred Sutton (MacDonald, op. cit., pp. 191-192) the amounts the Doolin gang obtained in their largest robberies, did not include the Canadian, Texas affair."

Arrington tracked the fugitives from Canadian into Oklahoma Territory, following the same tracks all the way to their hideout.

ATTORNEY: How could you do it?

"One of the horses was shod and three unshod."

ATTORNEY: You saw the tracks of the men at the stock pens? Did you measure any of these tracks?

"I saw the tracks. No, I didn't measure them. Three of the men had overshoes on. One had a small foot."

ATTORNEY: What size boot do you think he wore?

"About a 5 or 5½. High heel."

Isaacs' petition for release from jail was denied. He appealed the decision to the Court of Criminal Appeals of Texas on June 26, 1895. His attorneys were Plemons & Nial and Hodges & Jackson.

Mann Trice, assistant attorney general, prosecuted for the State.

Isaacs' appeal was denied on the ground that "a stenographic report of the evidence will not be considered as a statement of facts, being a violation of the rules of the Court of Criminal Appeals. Because there is no proper statement of facts in the case, there is no evidence . . . that can be considered. The judgment is affirmed."

Isaacs remained in jail.

Trial was held October 31, 1895, in Hardeman County. Isaacs was sentenced to life imprisonment at Huntsville, Texas, and he entered the state penitentiary on August 11, 1897. His number was 15531. Arrington took Isaacs to Huntsville. Cap, a relatively small man, had Isaacs handcuffed to his wrist. Arrington's young son, John, trailed behind them on their way to the train from the Canadian jail. John used to say that Cap was "worried because George was much bigger" and could have caused trouble. Apparently, George didn't.

Although the records at Huntsville were rather skimpy, a photostatic copy of his prison file showed he entered jail wearing a gold watch valued at $300 and $4.05 in cash. He was 39 years old, born in 1858, was 5 feet, 7 inches tall and weighed 140 pounds. His father was born in Georgia and his mother in Tennessee. His complexion was dark, eyes were blue and his hair gray. His habits were temperate, education poor but he was able to read and write.

He wore a size six shoe. He had a circle cut scar between the right forefinger and thumb and a 2½ inch scar diagonally across his forehead.

Isaacs wasn't in prison long. A notation in a ledger shows that he "escaped" and was never apprehended. One prison official suggested that "some grease" was applied where it counted. The story circulated around Canadian was that someone produced a forged pardon or had someone slip a pardon among the pile signed by the governor. No matter which. Isaacs was released.

He fled to Mexico and may have returned to Canadian to attend the funeral of his mother. He then went to Arizona and was never heard of again.

BIBLIOGRAPHY

Chapter Six

Habeas Corpus hearing, Hemphill County, Canadian, Texas.

Six-Gun and Silver Star, Glenn Shirley, University of New Mexico Press, Albuquerque, N.M., 1955.

Southwestern Reporter, Volume 31, Page 641.

Texas State Penitentiaries Records, obtained through cooperation of Henry R. Small, Bureau of Records and Identification, Huntsville, Texas.

The Canadian Free Press, various issues, 1889, obtained from microfilm in the Panhandle-Plains Museum, Canyon, Texas.

THE ARRINGTON HOME south of Canadian, Tex.

CAP ARRINGTON'S cabin on the Washita River. Photo taken in 1926 by J. Evetts Haley, Canyon, Tex. Photo is property of the Nita Stewart Haley Memorial Library.

81

EPILOGUE

Some Things Personal

Arrington was a cautious man. He was afraid of nothing, but he had made enemies during his long career in law enforcement, and he never placed himself in a position where he could be approached from behind or surprised face on.

It was rare for him to be without a gun. If he were not wearing one, he had one within easy reaching distance. He always knew where his weapons were. When in the barber's chair, he had his sixshooter in his hand under the barber's cloth. He locked his home up tight at night, and after nearly being shot through his front door, he never answered late-evening knocks without checking to see who his visitor was first. He never made the same mistake twice.

Arrington was a harsh man, but fair. He judged his visitors on the spot, and if he did not like what he saw, he had little to do with them. Being invited into his den was a mark of distinction and a sign that he liked you.

His home included a game room, and his study included his books, guns and whiskey. To be invited into this inner sanctum was an honor indeed.

George Washington Arrington married Miss Sarah (Sallie) Caroline Burnette on Oct. 18, 1883, in Westboro, Mo. He was 39 and she, 21. They moved to Mobeetie, Tex. that same year, where he was living while sheriff of Wheeler County.

Two of their children, John and Sadie, were born in the old jail in Mobeetie. Part of the two story structure was used as a residence.

Mrs. Arrington, born in Coke County, Tenn., May 2, 1862, moved with her parents to Iowa in 1869 and to Westboro in 1873. She was a charter member of the First Baptist Church in Canadian, Tex., and was active in the Women's Christian Temperance Union. She died June 1, 1945.

The Arringtons had three sons and six daughters: Gilbert, French, John, May, Sadie, Empress, Inez, Orlean and Caroline. Gilbert preceded his mother in death, and French died in 1973. John died in 1964. The daughters are now Mrs. May Grimes, Claude, Tex.; Mrs. Sadie Teas, Canadian, Tex.; Mrs. Empress Wolcott, Snyder, Tex.; Mrs. Inez Crenshaw, Daytona Beach, Fla.; Mrs. Orlean Hoghland, Perryton, Tex.; and Mrs. Caroline Long, Sedona, Ariz.

Arrington was a Mason and a member of the Moslah Shrine Temple in Fort Worth, Tex. He was an active member of the Cattle

Raisers of Texas for several years.

Arrington, who suffered from arthritis, used to go to Mineral Wells for the hot baths. He would stay there for the winter months. While returning home aboard a train from Mineral Wells, he suffered a heart attack, and was taken to his home in Canadian. He died in bed March 31, 1923. Burial was handled by the Stickley Funeral Home of Canadian.

Three thousand dollars was donated by friends for a monument for his grave. T.D. Hobart of Pampa and D.J. Young, president of the First National Bank, Canadian, collected the funds.

F.R. Jamison said of the fund raising, "The life thus sought to be revered through voluntary acts of his friends is regarded as a splendid privilege and will mark the sacred couch of one who carved upon the Indian infested region of Texas a habitude where today culture and refinement delights multiplied thousands." It is a fitting eulogy for a man who made a lasting mark on the Texas Panhandle.

Both Mr. and Mrs. Arrington are buried in Mobeetie.

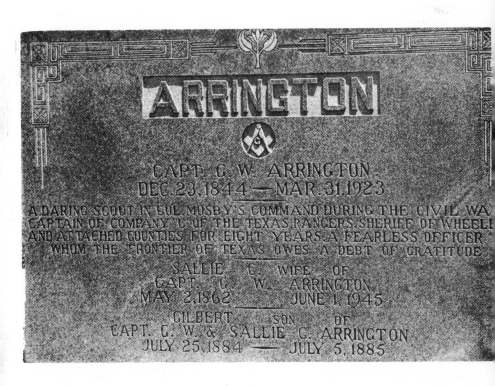

ARRINGTON

CAPT. G. W. ARRINGTON
DEC. 23, 1844 — MAR. 31, 1923

A DARING SCOUT IN COL. MOSBY'S COMMAND DURING THE CIVIL WAR
CAPTAIN OF COMPANY C OF THE TEXAS RANGERS. SHERIFF OF WHEELER
AND ATTACHED COUNTIES FOR EIGHT YEARS. A FEARLESS OFFICER
WHOM THE FRONTIER OF TEXAS OWES A DEBT OF GRATITUDE

SALLIE C. WIFE OF
CAPT. G. W. ARRINGTON
MAY 2, 1862   JUNE 1, 1945

GILBERT   SON   OF
CAPT. G. W. & SALLIE C. ARRINGTON
JULY 25, 1884 — JULY 5, 1885

MISCELLANEOUS LETTERS

W.B. Palmer Co.
Commission Merchants
No. 1321 Cary Street
Richmond, Va.
January 20, 1905

Dear Comrade:

I herewith enclose you your Cross of Honor handed me last night by the Daughters of the Confederacy. I would have my name engraved on this, the Daughters suggest this, and I have no doubt you can have this done in your place.

Yours very truly,
W. Ben Palmer

George W. Arrington, Esq.   Charlotteville, Va.
Canadian, Texas   December 29th, 1904

My dear old Comrade:

I have letters from both John W. Munson and Dr. John Wittshon asking me to write an account of the Bonham fight in which you and myself did the fighting after Charley Wittshon and George Gill were shot. I desire that you correct or approve what I have written, a copy of which I will send to you when I hear from you. You will recall that Bod Eastham remained in the lane, or road, while all the others were shooting in the yard. The reports published have been so inaccurate that these old comrades, along with John Gill (cousin of George Gill, killed), I desire the facts in this fight. Munson, as you know, doubtless is writing articles in the Munsey's Magazine of Mosby's Command, and before writing about the fight in which Pom Gill and Wiltshire were fatally wounded, desire you and myself to give the facts, and you to correct my statement where I am in error, or to corroborate it as you remember this encounter.

Many years have elapsed since then, but it is still fresh in my memory, and will ever be. Two of McDick Tillotson's nephews, the Brown boys, are engaged in the drug business in this city, and one of them gave me a photo of yourself taken in 1877. Would you like this to appear with the article? When I remember you as a soldier, you were like myself, a mere smooth-faced young man. The photo shows you to be possessed of a long beard, but time has brought many changes since then for we are fast getting to be old men. And many of our old Command have already crossed over the river. Wiltshire thinks you told him once that his brother Charley, while lying on the ground, raised himself to his elbow and fired a

84

parting shot at Ferris as he passed out of the gate. He desires this to appear also if he remembers you correctly, and that Ferris returned the fire. I was in the Wilson Camp at this time, where I went after emptying my one revolver, to borrow another from Bob Eastham, which I did, and with which in company with yourself, we pursued the two Yankees into the Yankee camp.

I hope I shall hear from you promptly and fully. With best wishes for the New Year and the hope that you will visit your friend in old Virginia one of these days again.

I am Yours Sincerely,
Bartlett Bolling

Tennessee Confederate Soldiers Home
Nashville, Tennessee
27th February 1903

Dear Mr. Arrington:

A letter from one of "Ours"—Mosby's Cavalry—informed us on inquiry of your whereabouts, hence it gives me hope to get in touch with you once more. You, of whom I have spoken so deservedly as one of the very bravest of the 43rd Virginia Cavalry Rangers. You may remember we boarded awhile at Dick Littleton's when Miss Thompson and Miss Nettie Campbell were visiting there. I remember your fine horses, the chestnut and the gray. I have been here about a year now, having rheumatism—that ailment has vanished; I feel physically and mentally as efficient as when thirty-five, and could ride and shoot as well as ever should a return of volunteers be in demand in this approaching war in Warsaw.

I anticipate leaving in the Spring to teach again, my line in former times. My specialty, French, is as fluent as ever. I have taught in public schools from Maryland and Virginia through the states to Texas and Indian Territory. French I acquired in Paris, Military Preparatory College. Here at the C. Home we have the necessaries of existence, yet I pant for active life again. We receive no money at all except from some practical outside friends now and then. I desire to reach Texas again. Had I the money I would proceed at once. I'll make the trip in spite of impetuosity ere long. Best wishes to you. Kindly write as soon as convenient. John Puryear is near—his address, Gordonsville, Va.

Ever yours in kind remembrances, dear John C. Orrick of Alabama,

J.A. Richardson

1519 20th Street, N.W.
Washington, D.C.
February 2, 1910

My dear Arrington:

The Mosby man at the Library of Congress is Capt. Dunnington of E Co. I introduced myself to him and showed him the two small pictures I have of you and the family group. He was very much pleased. He brought out the book published in 1909 on Mosby and his Men, and in it is the small picture of you (Bloomfield), your handsome self, and a very interesting account of your valiant and gallant services. Last night I attended a meeting of the Confederate Camp #171 here, and met Mr. Robert M. Hanover and Mr. Throop, who remembered you well and affectionately. I showed them the picture of you and family. They sent you kindest regards and congratulate you upon looking so well, and having such a fine looking family.

This afternoon I called on Colonel Mosby at his room, 1333 L Street, NW, and introduced myself as an old friend of his gallant soldier, John C. Orrick, and showed him the family group. His face lit up with pleasure and he said many good things of you. He asked me to write you to say that he has never forgotten you and to give you his kindest regards and best wishes. He is looking very well and says that he never enjoyed better health. He is an assistant attorney in U.S. Department of Justice here. He did say that he had never met General Stoughton after the war. You no doubt remember the time he yanked him out of bed and sent him to Richmond.*

I suppose you have the book published last year. If not, you should order it. Colonel Mosby has written a very fine book, "Stuart's Cavalry in the Gettysburg Campaign." It is spoken of very highly. I will read it at the Library. I enclose the publisher's advertisement. Col. Mosby gave it to me. I send it to you as a momento from him. The picture of the Colonel on it is as you remember him. The rooms of the Confederate Camp #171 here are at 1322 Vermont Avenue, and the walls are covered with our dear old flags and pictures of our heroes. At every meeting there are talks and papers read on stirring war subjects. You might send them a chapter out of the book of your varied experiences. I will write you

---

* Grayson is referring to one of Mosby's most spectacular exploits during his guerilla career. On March 8, 1863, Mosby captured Brigadier General Edwin H. Stoughton at Fairfax Court House, 10 miles from Washington. Mosby and 29 followers slipped through the pickets guarding the town and entered the house where Stoughton was sleeping off a drunk. Mosby pulled off the bedclothes, whacked the general on his bare rump and told him he was a prisoner. He delivered Stoughton, two captains and 30 enlisted men to the Confederate Army.

again when I see other Mosby men. I hope you have ere this all four of the Benson books.

Affectionately yours,
S. Monroe Grayson

General V.Y. Cook
Dear Sir:
I have the honor to acknowledge the receipt of your letter dated 2/15/1907, offering me position on your staff. I enlisted April 13, 1861 and was mustered into the Confederate service in May in Co. D, 5th Alabama Infantry in Va. After the Seven Days Fight in front of Richmond, I joined Co. 3, Jeff Davis Legion, Houston's Brigade of Cavalry, and afterwards transferred to Co. C, 43rd Va. Battalion, Cavalry, Col. Jno. S. Mosby, commanding. I was paroled April 29th, 1865. I held no commission in the Confederate Army. My title of Captain was given me by the Governor of Texas in the Battalion of Texas Rangers in the '70's, when I commanded a company for three years and seven days on the Texas frontier and the Mexican border.
I highly appreciate the honor you do me in tending me the position on your staff, and regret that my health will not permit me to accept, as I am a great sufferer from rheumatism.
Again thanking you, I am yours respectfully,

G.W. Arrington

M.M. French
Notary Public, Real Estate & Insurance
Canadian, Texas

Captain D.E. Grove:
This will introduce Capt. G.W. Arrington of this County, formerly of Alabama, a man of distinction as a Confederate soldier, and also as Captain of Texas Rangers for a number of years.
Treat him as a person worthy of all the best you can extend. I take this liberty of introducing Capt. Arrington, feeling that two such spirits can while away an hour or two pleasantly in reviewing old war times. In spirit, I will be with you all during the Reunion, and indulge in reminiscences of a period of our lives dear to us all.

Very Truly yours,
M.M. French*

---

* Cap Arrington's son, French, was named for M.M. French, a close friend.

G.W. ARRINGTON was a Mason and a member of the Samson
Lodge #231, Highlands (then Lynchburg), Tex.; Fort Griffin Lodge
#489 (now Throckmorton, Tex.); Albany Lodge #482; and Miami
(Tex.) Lodge #805.